WELCOME TO YOUR PERIOD!

STRIPES PUBLISHING LIMITED
An imprint of the Little Tiger Group
1 Coda Studios, 189 Munster Road,
London SW6 6AW

www.littletiger.co.uk

Originally published in Australia by Hardie Grant Egmont in 2019

First published in Great Britain by Stripes Publishing Limited in 2020
Text copyright © Yumi Stynes & Dr Melissa Kang, 2019
Illustration copyright © Jenny Latham, 2019
Series design copyright © Hardie Grant Egmont, 2019

ISBN: 978-1-78895-294-1

Printed and bound in China.

STP/1800/0464/0122

2 4 6 8 10 9 7 5 3

YUMI STYNES & DR MELISSA KANG

WELCOME TO YOUR PERIOD!

LITTLE TIGER

LONDON

To the next generation of bleeders, may you kick ass and have many laughs, and to their mothers, who try to protect their children from all pain but fail, and fail gloriously.

Yumi

To Julian, Samantha, Georgia and Hannah-Rose, who learnt a lot of stuff but taught me more.

Melissa

How do you use this book?

Short answer – any way you like!

Let's start by saying that it is *totally OK* to be excited or scared or nervous about getting your period. **Of COURSE.** It's all new, right? But no matter what your situation, this book will give you the info you need to handle your period like a boss.

There's a lot in here, and you don't need to get your head around every bit of it right away. You can read this book cover to cover or dip in to find the most interesting bits.

You probably just want to get to the stuff that you need to know right now.

If you're starting from scratch and want to know what a period even IS, go to **THE BASICS** on page 4.

If you want to know the difference between pads and tampons (and how to use them), go to page 42.

And if you're interested in what's happening behind the scenes in your body, check out page 122 and 148.

There's also a vocab section on page 154 in case you need a refresher!

Over the next few years, the things you want to know will change. That's OK – this book will still be here when you need it. Pages you didn't think you needed to read will suddenly become relevant.

And when you feel like you're a period boss, you can share this book with your sister, cousin or friend and say,

"Welcome to your period! Guess what? It's going to be **totally fine.**"

Contents

Welcome TO YOUR Period

Hi!

So glad you're here. WELCOME to your period!

Listen, I want to tell you something **(this is Yumi speaking)**. When I was a kid growing up in Australia, it was tricky finding honest info about periods. But the one place you could go was a column in *Dolly* (a magazine for teenagers) called **Dolly Doctor**.

Dolly Doctor was a regular Q&A with a real doctor who specialized in girl problems. You could write in to ask her advice, and she never laughed at the questions, or made fun of you, or even flinched – no matter WHAT you asked. Best of all, her answers were spot-on 100 per cent of the time!

If you had told me that one day I would be co-writing a book with Dolly Doctor about periods, I would have screamed with disbelief and happiness!

> **I look up to her, I trust her and I am so thrilled to introduce her to you by her real name: Dr Melissa Kang.**

Even though she is totally up on the science now, periods were a complete mystery to Dr Melissa when she first got hers. (And they were to me too.)

To learn about periods, Dr Melissa had to watch an excruciating video at school in Year Seven. Everyone in the class was so embarrassed; they couldn't say anything or even look at each other. After that, her mum had ONE talk with her about periods and that was it.

My own mum wordlessly handed me a free leaflet written by a pad manufacturer and that was pretty much our 'talk' about periods – but to tell you the truth, I wasn't too fazed. I secretly thought I probably wouldn't get my period, at all, ever – because I *really* didn't want to, so why should I?!

Later, Dr Melissa and I found out that a lot of girls feel the same way. And as we matured, we both wanted to be more open about periods, learn as much as we could, and talk about them without shame. Getting your period is not only natural and really common but also pretty interesting!

As an adult, Dr Melissa spent more than 20 years writing the Dolly Doctor advice columns. She received – and answered – thousands of real-life letters from people like you! We've included some of them in this book and, yes, they're real too.

Unlike Dr Melissa, I'm not an expert. But I do have a good memory, and I remember that even if you already know heaps about periods, getting your first one can be a little bit daunting – maybe scary, maybe exciting, but always ... *something*. So when it comes to periods, there's no such thing as a silly question. Regular, irregular, painful, painless, heavy, light – everyone's periods are different. **So – WELCOME!** This book will arm you with facts and rock-solid info so you can handle your period like a boss.

We hope it will help you feel confident as you get to know your body.

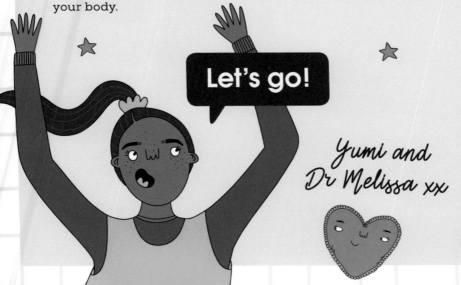

Let's go!

Yumi and Dr Melissa xx

THE BASICS

Fallopian tube

Uterus

Lining

Ovary

Cervix

Vagina

What actually is a period?

A period is a natural bleed that comes out of the vagina about once a month, usually lasting about five days. It is literally the shedding of the lining of your uterus – periodically. It's also known as menstruation.

It's as simple as that and, trust us, you will be able to handle it.

Who gets a period?

If you have a uterus, you will most likely get your period!

When is it coming?

Your first period occurs as part of puberty (for more on puberty, see page 122). The average age to start getting your period is between 12½ and 13 years. But the boundaries are wide! You can be as young as 10 or as old as 15, and some people will start even earlier or later.

Most of the time, there are some signs that your first period is coming. Turn to page 151 to learn more.

How long does it go on for?

The actual bleed

For most adolescents, the bleeding part lasts two to seven days, with an average of around five days.

The cycle

Your cycle is counted from the first day of your period when you bleed to the first day of your *next* period. It can take a couple of years for your cycle to find its own pattern. It's usually around 28–32 days, with variations from person to person, and month to month. Teenagers can have even bigger variations (21–45 days). For more on your cycle, see page 148.

In life

Once you start getting your period, you tend to get it for the next 30 to 40 years, interrupted by pregnancy and childbirth (if you have kids), until menopause. Menopause is when your reproductive system shuts down and you can no longer make a baby in your body. The average age for a person to reach menopause is 51 years old.

QUESTIONS FOR DR MELISSA

I'm scared!

> **I am a 12-year-old girl and I am terrified of getting my period. What do I do to calm myself down?**

A lot of people feel scared about getting their period for the first time. If this is you, we promise **YOU ARE NOT THE ONLY ONE.** Of course it's OK to be scared. To you, it's an unknown. The best thing you can do when you're scared of something is to find out more about it. That means you're doing the right thing by reading this book!

Look around. Almost all the adult women you see in the world have experienced menstruation. And they have survived. And they have gone on to kick ass.

Take a deep breath. You are going to be OK!

MANAGING FEELINGS OF FEAR

1. Take deep breaths.
2. Know what it is you are fearful of.
3. Go for a walk.
4. Take a big drink of water.
5. Find someone to talk about it with.
6. Realize that you are not alone.

Does it hurt?

Not that much to begin with, especially for the first few months.

As you get older, period pain can become more common, although the feeling is different for everyone. If you do get some pain from your period, it can feel like heaviness, or a sort of muscle cramp behind where the elastic waistband of your underpants sits. Pain is not actually caused by the bleeding out of the vagina, but comes from muscle contractions of the uterus, which is higher up.

I didn't even notice my first period. It was completely painless, and was just a few brown streaks on my underpants over about three days. It was actually my grandmother who told me, because she'd noticed it when she was doing the family's laundry! Some people might find that embarrassing, but for me it was easier talking to my grandma about it than anyone else. *Dr Melissa*

If you're just starting out with your period or haven't had one yet, pain is probably not something you need to worry about right now. For more on period pain, see page 96.

As well as the flow of blood, I sometimes feel tenderness on my labia (or 'outer lips'), as though I've got a bruise down there. The feeling lasts for about a day. Some of my friends get tummy cramps, or feel a bit achy below the bellybutton. *Yumi*

Why do you get periods?

AKA "Why is blood lining my uterus when it never used to be there?!"

As you enter puberty, your body kicks off a magical combination of hormone shifts and physical growth that causes your uterus to start growing a new lining of blood and other fluids. It's there to help a baby grow, and in the absence of pregnancy, your body wants to get rid of that lining, or 'shed' it. Shedding is what we also describe as bleeding. It's all to do with the reproductive system, which you can learn more about on page 148.

Once you've had a period and the lining is gone for the month, your uterus starts accumulating a fresh lining all over again, which it will get rid of the next time around.

I think of it as an empty room. In puberty, the walls, floor and ceiling are lined with lovely red upholstery. Then we chuck out the upholstery and start again. *Yumi*

How much blood comes out?

It may feel (and look) like a lot, but it isn't really – around four or five teaspoons over the first two to three days of bleeding. You can use pads, tampons and other menstrual products to capture it – we've covered all your options on page 42.

These first few days are usually described as your 'heaviest' days, because that's when the most fluid comes out (about 75–90 per cent of the total blood loss). After that, the flow tapers off, becoming lighter and lighter until it stops. That really light flow at the end of your period leaves spots of blood on your underwear or on the pad, which is why it's sometimes called 'spotting'.

Where does my period come out of?

Your period comes out of your vagina, which is not the same as where your wee comes from. Your vagina is about two centimetres below your urethra (your wee hole), and three centimetres above your anus (your bum hole).

For more on your vagina, see page 120.

Why do periods come monthly? Is it to do with the moon?

Although periods and full moons each come around about once a month, the timing of the two seems to be just a coincidence. In adults, the average time from period to period is 28 days, but can be anywhere between 24 and 35 days. For young teens it can be anywhere from 21 to 45 days. We call this a 'cycle', and we count it from the first day of getting your period to the first day of your next one.

What does it look like?

When you first start getting your period, it is often brown or black in colour, and sometimes just looks like streaks on your pants or pad. Once periods are established and more regular, the flow is usually a dark red during heavier days and can become brown as the period gets lighter. It varies from person to person, and period to period.

Which underwear is best to wear when you've got your period?

Wear what feels most comfortable for you! If you're wearing a pad you might find that a wider gusset (the bit that sits between your legs, under your vagina) is more supportive, like a boy-leg brief. A g-string probably isn't going to cut it!

Can anyone tell if I have my period?

NO-ONE WILL KNOW THAT YOU HAVE YOUR PERIOD UNLESS YOU TELL THEM.

What will it feel like?

It feels like you have a small amount of wetness between your legs. But not *exactly* like you've wet your pants. For starters, what comes out is stickier than wee, and you also can't control the blood flow by tightening your pelvic floor muscles (the same muscles you use to stop and start weeing).

Having blood in your pants can get a bit messy, so most people wear a pad or use a tampon or menstrual cup when they have their period. If you're wearing a pad, the liquid will get absorbed so that you feel dry. If you are using a tampon or menstrual cup, you don't feel anything at all until they are full. See page 42 for more information about these menstrual products.

It's important to know that the flow of your period comes from your vagina, not your urethra (where urine comes from). When you have your period, you can sometimes feel a warm liquid coming out of your vagina, but it's a once-in-a-while type of sensation, not a constant stream.

Seeing blood in your pants for the first time can be a bit confronting, but you'll get used to it! Even people who have been super-squeamish about the sight of blood end up being pretty calm about their periods. *Yumi*

I'm a young disabled girl; I sometimes use a wheelchair and my dexterity isn't great. The level of your disability is going to make a difference to how it affects your period, but it doesn't have to be a catastrophe. Talking to young girls who are about to get their period and are disabled, I think: don't worry about it – it doesn't have to be a terrible thing and it doesn't have to be that hard. *Stella, 19*

Let me know if you want to chat about it more before it comes!

OMG, that would be great 😊

I'M WORRIED IT WILL NEVER COME

You might be feeling as though **ALL** your friends have their period, and yours will never turn up. Or maybe you're keen to be first! But if your period hasn't arrived yet, when should you start getting worried?

The short answer is: not for a while. If your period is still a no-show, you don't need to start thinking about talking to a doctor until you're 15 or 16 years old – and even then things are likely to be fine. In the meantime, don't stress!

It might help put your mind at ease to ask your mum, sister, cousins, aunties or grandma about when they first got their periods.

EVERY BODY IS DIFFERENT.

You may discover that theirs came later, in which case yours could come later. Or you might find out that some of your family's periods started earlier, and some started later, which isn't that helpful! It's anyone's guess when yours will arrive, although you do get some clues from your own body – see page 92.

If you don't have the right family member to ask, talk to someone at school – a trusted teacher, a school nurse or a counsellor. Try not to worry about being embarrassed – periods may seem scary or mortifying before they first start, but most adults with uteruses are used to getting them. After a few months, they don't seem like such a big deal anymore. (Before you know it, **YOU** will be offering advice to younger friends and family!)

I was almost 13 when I got my first period. I think my mum had been around the same age too, and it was the same for my younger sister. *Dr Melissa*

16

SEEING A DOCTOR

In many countries (including the UK), adolescents have the legal right to see a doctor confidentially. This means a doctor needs to ask YOU for permission to discuss things with your parent or carer, and you have the right to say no.

The only time they can break that agreement is if your immediate safety is at risk – this is really important for keeping you safe.

If the doctor believes you are sufficiently mature, they can prescribe treatments without parental consent.

For most adolescents, it's a gradual process – when you're very young, you probably *want* to involve your parents or carer. But as you get older, you might want more privacy and to take more responsibility for your health care. It can also depend on how useful it is to have the support of your parent or carer.

IT CAN BE HELPFUL TO ASK YOUR DOCTOR ABOUT THE PROS AND CONS OF INVOLVING A PARENT IN YOUR CARE.

BEFORE YOU GET YOUR PERIOD

Being prepared for something that's never happened to you before is tricky, right?

Luckily, there ARE some things you can do to prepare for your first period:

1. Sort out your period pack.

Having your supplies on hand will help you feel ready for anything! To learn what goes into your period pack, see page 20.

2. Try on a pad.

Place the sticky side of the pad down on to your pants, underneath your vagina. Pull your pants up and then walk around. (Go to page 42 for more guidance.) How does it feel? Pat your bum – can you feel it? Put your outfit back on and take a look in the mirror – can you see the pad through your clothes? Probably not, right?

3. Buy black pants.

Black pants are way better than light-coloured ones for hiding leaks and spills (and trust us, leaks and spills are going to happen from time to time). We recommend phasing in LOTS of black ones – you might feel more comfortable wearing these on heavier days.

4. Talk about it!

Ask your friends and the other period bosses in your life about their periods. We totally understand feeling a bit shy about it, but from experience we reckon you can always find a couple of menstruating adults who are up for a period chat! They may be able to share their experiences and give you some basic advice.

5. Read a book!

The best thing about novels is that they allow you to experience something before it happens to you. Here are some of our favourite books that actually deal with periods in a meaningful way:

⭐ **The Last One in the Universe**
by Chrissie Perry

⭐ **Are You There God? It's Me, Margaret**
by Judy Blume

⭐ **To Night Owl from Dogfish**
by Holly Goldberg Sloan
and Meg Wolitzer

AND OF COURSE, READ THIS BOOK! KNOWLEDGE IS POWER.

I talked to two of my cousins and to my best friend. They knew heaps about periods from their mothers, ages before they got them, and shared that with me. We still collectively freaked out before any of us got our first period, but once we did, it was like, 'Oh! That's not so bad after all.' *Dr Melissa*

BE PREPARED WITH A PERIOD PACK

One thing that will help you feel ready for your period is having a **PERIOD PACK** in your bag!

A period pack is a small, zipped-up bag of everything you need for your period. It comes with you everywhere, so you don't get stuck somewhere with no supplies. A small pencil case or pouch is the perfect size – something discreet that doesn't take up much room, and that you feel comfortable pulling out of your carry bag, schoolbag or handbag when you need it.

This is one of the reasons many adult ladies carry handbags. Handbags are basically glorified period packs. *Yumi*

My daughter got hers at 12 years old. At her school you have to go to the toilet in pairs, so she was with a friend. She sat down on the loo and saw a little bit of blood on her pants, and shouted out, "I think I got my period!" Her friend went, "Right, I'll go get supplies." She went to her bag, gathered up a few other friends and they all grabbed their period stashes and came back and gave her the options.
Cymone, 45

Your period pack should include:

Menstrual products

Whether you prefer pads or tampons, include three in your pack. If you're not sure yet, pads are a good place to start, but it's also nice to keep a spare tampon in there. They don't take up much space, and one of your friends – or a stranger – might ask you for one. (It always feels good to help out in a period emergency!) To learn more about your options and how to use pads, tampons and more, see page 42.

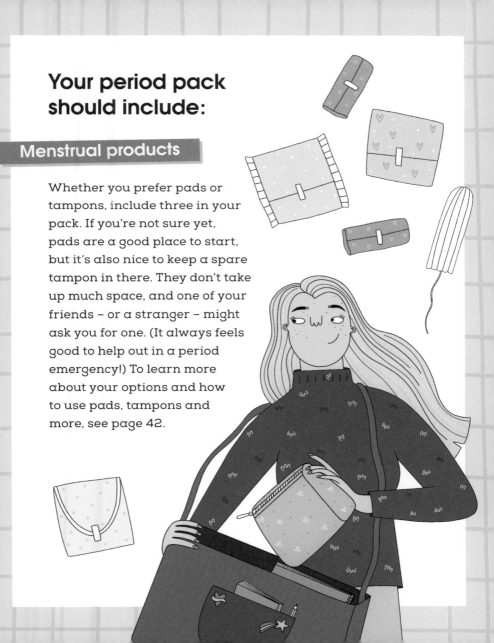

Spare pants

It's a good idea to keep these in a ziplock bag. If you have a period bleed on your pants then you can swap them for the clean pair and pop the stained ones into the ziplock bag to be washed when you get home.

> I bring a small bag to carry pads, tampons and panty liners. OH MY GOSH, I only recently learnt to put spare pants in there! If it's your first, second or third day of your period, always put spare pants in there. If it's your fourth day, don't bother. *Tans. 13*

Depending on how you feel when you get your period, in time you may add the following:

Pain medication

If you sometimes take pain medication like ibuprofen or paracetamol for your period, add two tablets to your period pack.

Emergency chocolate

Just in case, because chocolate is yum.

Keep your period pack handy so that you can easily grab it at school, on your way home, out with friends or at your after-school job. A special little bag might seem a bit fancy or fussy, but we **strongly recommend** it because your period supplies can get really beaten up if they're bouncing around loose inside your schoolbag. Or they might jump out of your bag when you're not looking!

I used to host a live TV show where a LOT could go wrong – so to make myself feel more secure, I would wear two pairs of underpants! It made me feel more in control. A good period pack should make you feel the same way. Protected. Secure. Like, babe, I've got this! *Yumi*

I'm a big fan of the rollercoaster of emotions you experience when your period surprises you ('Oh no!'), but then you remember you're prepared ('Oh yes!'). Possibly the only better feeling is when you're in a bathroom and a stranger asks you for a tampon or a pad, and you can swoop in to save their day. *Penny, 33*

What about at home?

What's the home version of a period pack? Good question! It's somewhere handy you can stash all your supplies, like in your bathroom or bedroom. If you live with your mum and she gets her period, suss out what she does and go along with that.

You can either keep your supplies all together in a small bag or just put the packets of pads or tampons somewhere within reach. The closer to the toilet, the easier it will be to get them when your period arrives – so you can either leave them out nearby or, if you prefer, just in the nearest cupboard.

In my house, I keep a couple of packets of pads and tampons by the toilet at all times. I don't put them away in the cupboard – they're just out there in the open where everyone can see them. No-one minds. Getting your period is normal!

And since menstrual products should never be flushed down the toilet, I also make sure there's a bin next to the toilet. That way no-one has to take their used pad or tampon any further than a metre from the loo. *Yumi*

Dealing with your first period

Wow! OK. So after all the build-up, it actually happened! You sat down to use the toilet, discovered something red or brown in your pants, and now you've got your period. Congratulations!

So what do you do now?

I was at home, sitting on the toilet, and then blood came out. I was like, **Uuuuuuhm, WHAT IS THIS?** I freaked out and asked my mum. I think I was in Grade Seven, and **I had NO IDEA about periods.** I was not expecting it. None of my friends had really talked about it. I did have a couple of friends who had got their periods before me, but it was a cultural thing that we didn't really talk about it – it was a very private, very personal thing. *Hsin-Ju, 34*

Find a pad

If you're lucky, you'll have your period pack ready to go in your bag, no matter where you are (although if you're really, **REALLY** lucky, you'll be at home). Take out a pad, unwrap it, stick it in your pants, and then feel like you have a special secret for the rest of the day.

Or you might like to tell some friends about it, and you can all make a bit of a fuss over this exciting milestone!

A few hours later, you'll need to change the pad by taking out the old one, wrapping it up in toilet paper and putting it in a bin or sanitary disposal unit, then putting a new one in your underpants.

If you don't have your period pack with you, fold up some toilet paper and tuck that into your pants instead. If your pants are snug, it should be fine for an hour or so. Then tell a friend, a teacher or a trusted adult, and they should be able to help you out with some pads until you get home.

It was night-time, and I went to the toilet and found that I had just got my period. I was confused about what to do next. My mum was out, but my older sister helped me with a pad. My older sister gives me so much help with things like managing cramps, stains and feeling sick. *Chloe, 16*

Tell the people at home!

So, now that it's here, it's a good idea to tell someone, even if it feels awkward. Be brave! Your mum, dad, older sister or main carer will want to know, as they'll be the ones helping you to buy pads, tampons, cups or period pants in the future. And also, this is **GOOD** news. You're growing up! Your body is doing the things it's meant to do! Chances are they'll be super glad for you.

Smile to yourself

Your period came! Look at yourself in the mirror. **WHO IS THIS** amazing person looking back and taking more steps towards becoming a grown-up?

You're not alone if your first period is a bit anticlimactic! My first couple of periods weren't even red – they were a murky sort of brown and a bit watery. I was hoping it'd be more like a murder scene and instead it was like Shrek's swamp. *Yumi*

I was in Grade Seven and discovered it when I went to the bathroom after school. I called my mum at work, and she was like, "OH MY GOD, THAT'S SO EXCITING!" Then she called out to her entire office and shouted, "My daughter's got her period!" Deeply, deeply embarrassing. I was fine for Mum to know but I didn't expect the whole world to know! *Audrey, 37*

I remember when I first got my period, I just walked into my sister's room, grabbed a tampon and did what I had to do! Then I walked downstairs and said to my mum, "I got my period," and she asked if I had something to take care of it. I said, "Yeah, I got a tampon out of Danielle's room," and then my sister got angry with me for going into her room without asking! *Nicole, 40*

All my friends started getting it and I was kind of late compared to them so I thought I was really ready for it, but it was still a shock and really overwhelming! Straight away I went to my mum and I was really nervous to tell her – I don't know why – and I said, "Mum, I think I got my period!" And she was like, "That's wonderful!" And I was like, "No, it's not!" *Kiara, 15*

WAYS TO BREAK THE NEWS

Hey, Mum, guess what? I failed maths! Just kidding, I got my period.

Mum, can you come in here and have a look at this?

Dad, I got my period!

Hey, Dad, we'll have to start buying pads for a while. I mean, forever.

Hey, bestie, I got my period for the first time!

YOU GOT IT!

Celebrate with a period party!

Getting your period for the first time is a huge milestone, and it only happens once. So you might feel like seizing the moment and celebrating!

Whether you're throwing the period party for yourself, your best friend or sibling, here are some great ideas to welcome the very first period:

Tie red and white balloons to the front fence. No-one has to know why, but the red is for blood and the white is for the pads you use to manage the blood. It can be like a secret joke or a big, loud announcement.

Hang out with your friends and make mugs of ginger tea and mini sandwiches, and talk about the first time THEY got their periods. Then maybe settle down to binge-watch your favourite show together.

You might really want to get into the theme by serving red food, like red velvet cake!

PERIOD PARTY

Have a ladies-only party and invite your favourite relatives, like aunties, cousins and sisters. If you want, they can all talk about the first time they got their period, or you can just get on with the important business of making each other laugh.

We were very open about periods – we actually threw little parties for each other! We basically just got each other presents. I remember when I got mine, I got a pair of Kookai underpants that were sort of like boxers – which I really liked because they were sort of androgynous – and a Sudoku book. *Nevo, 22*

You might prefer not to celebrate, and that's perfectly fine too. Why not curl up with a good book and not budge until you want to?

My mum was really excited and I think she said something like, "That's fantastic!" and gave me a hug. And then she got a pad for me and showed me how to use it. I think my mum made it a little bit of a low-key celebration between her and me. She let me know that it was something positive and lovely and important.

I definitely would follow a similar attitude as my mum and probably build on that from a traditional perspective as well. Because we lost a lot of our traditional Wiradjuri* culture, we'd want to keep this perspective of celebration and that it's a very important milestone in a woman's life. I can imagine that it could be so many things, but if it's framed in the right way, it's very empowering.

Samantha, 30

* the Wiradjuri people are a group of Australian Aboriginal people

I was 13 when I got my period for the first time. As my underwear got dirty, I showed it to my mother and confirmed it. As a custom of Japan, we celebrated by cooking red rice (sticky rice with red beans in it), like it was a birthday. *Itsuko, 55*

If you feel comfortable, have a regular party with all your friends (gender = irrelevant), and sing 'happy birthday' to your period. Everyone can bring gift-wrapped pads, tampons, period pants or menstrual cups!

I told my mum – she was really happy and took me out for dinner with my godmother. They sat there for hours and told stories about getting their periods and THAT WAS EVEN WORSE than getting my period! I found it really embarrassing to have to talk about those things! *Marisa, 33*

I CAN'T TALK ABOUT PERIODS WITH MY PARENTS

Talking about your period for the first time can be nerve-wracking, especially if you feel shy or embarrassed (which is totally normal – it's new!). But what happens if you try to raise the subject with your parents or carers at home, yet they just don't seem to want to talk about it?

Reasons might be:

* They don't want you to grow up.

* They literally don't know what to say.

* They're always working.

* They're always on their phone.

* They're embarrassed or shy when it comes to talking about periods.

* It hasn't occurred to them that you might be up to that stage in your life.

* Your mum, dad or carer has problems of their own that make it harder for them to focus on yours.

* There's a language barrier.

Whatever the reason your parents are tricky to communicate with, it's not your fault. When we were writing this book, we spoke to a lot of people who had parents who weren't great communicators on this topic – and they survived.

The fact that you have this book in your hands is a good sign. It means that the person who gave you this book cares, or that you care and are smart enough to seek out information and find solutions.

Dad, I need to talk to you about my period. I know it makes you uncomfortable – but this really needs to happen.

Mum, can we schedule some time to talk about the fact that I'll be getting my period soon, soon?

Mum. Mum, Mum, Mum, Mum. Listen. Periods. Me. Talk. Let's.

Here are some ways to start the conversation about periods at home:

You could write a note, send a calendar invitation via computer or send a text.

We think it's really important to have at least **ONE** person you can talk to about your period, so if it isn't going to be a parent, the first place to look is your wider family – aunties, sisters, trusted friends – and then your school. There will almost always be someone at school you can talk to about awkward stuff – and it's often someone who has had **SPECIAL TRAINING** in how to have those conversations! Ask to see the counsellor, the guidance expert, the year level coordinator, a female PE teacher, or just that teacher who's always had your back.

Beyond school, there are these fantastic people who know all about the human body – doctors and nurses!

THINK ABOUT THE BEST WAY TO GET THROUGH TO YOUR MUM OR DAD AND USE THAT METHOD OF COMMUNICATION TO START THE CONVERSATION.

1 NEW TXT

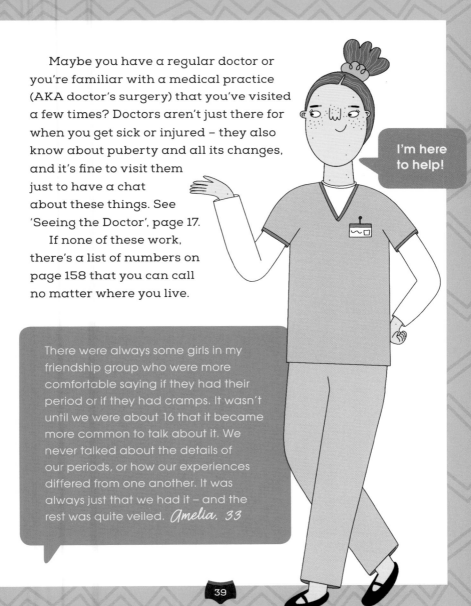

Maybe you have a regular doctor or you're familiar with a medical practice (AKA doctor's surgery) that you've visited a few times? Doctors aren't just there for when you get sick or injured – they also know about puberty and all its changes, and it's fine to visit them just to have a chat about these things. See 'Seeing the Doctor', page 17.

If none of these work, there's a list of numbers on page 158 that you can call no matter where you live.

I'm here to help!

There were always some girls in my friendship group who were more comfortable saying if they had their period or if they had cramps. It wasn't until we were about 16 that it became more common to talk about it. We never talked about the details of our periods, or how our experiences differed from one another. It was always just that we had it – and the rest was quite veiled. *Amelia, 33*

WHAT HAPPENS AFTER YOUR FIRST PERIOD?

Nothing much! You deal with it, and life goes on as normal. No-one looks at you like you're special, because no-one can tell anything is different unless you say something or have a period party.

Every month you will need to make sure your bathroom cupboard is stocked with period supplies. And don't worry if your periods aren't regular to begin with – they tend to settle into a predictable pattern after a year or so.

A lot of girls get their first period and then it doesn't happen again for a few months. This happened to me. I got a couple of weird periods about a month apart, then nothing for a couple of months and then it came a few more times, then nothing, and then it started to be pretty regular after that. *Yumi*

My second period came about four months after my first one. I began to wonder if the first one had been a dream. My cycle got regular only after about eight months. *Dr Melissa*

When I told my older sisters, they were like, "Whoo-hoo! You're a woman now, you're one of us!" *Nadine, 35*

I think because of all the hoo-ha around the first time you get your period I actually expected that I would wake up the next morning and be an accomplished woman! *Marihuzka, 36*

Basically, in traditional Indonesian culture (which is how my mum grew up) when a girl gets her period it's seen as a total transition into womanhood. Indonesian culture views having your period as powerful because you are now literally able to give life. There are so many customs that go along with having your period, like you can't visit any ancient temples while you're on your period or any places of sacred significance. This is because the energy is too powerful. They believe that blood energy belongs to the earth and that sacred sites such as temples have sky energy – and the two are not to be muddled. (Wild, I know!) *Amandah, 30*

HOW TO MANAGE YOUR PERIOD

Pads, tampons and more

There are lots of things you can use to manage your period like a boss. They're collectively referred to as **menstrual products** or **sanitary items**. Here are the most common ones and how to use them!

YOU CAN BUY TAMPONS AND PADS FROM SUPERMARKETS, CHEMISTS AND MOST SHOPS.

Pads

Pads are easy to use and you'll probably find them the best product to start with when you're new to having your period. (They're pretty good the rest of the time, too.) Pads have an adhesive strip that sticks to your pants, and they absorb period flow as it comes out of the vagina.

To use a pad, you just peel off the protective layer or wrapping, then press the sticky side on to the inside middle of your pants, underneath where your vagina sits. Once the pad is stuck down, pull up your pants and see how it feels.

Occasionally pads can leak (like if you have a heavy flow or you go too long without changing them). If there's going to be leakage, it's more likely to come from the back than the front, so try to favour a few extra centimetres of pad towards your bum.

Pads come in a few different lengths and thicknesses, so you might need to try a few sizes, shapes and brands until you find something you're comfortable with. Liners are similar to pads, and are for catching a very light flow or discharge, or for 'just in case' days.

My friend Lila prefers to use pads because it lets her see what's going on. She has a better idea of what is coming out of her body. *Yumi*

wings

Some pads come with 'wings', which wrap around underneath your pants. This is to stop your pants from getting reddy-brown marks on the sides if the pad bunches up a little when you walk around. It's up to you whether you want to use pads with wings or not.

THE USEFUL THING ABOUT PADS IS THAT WHEN YOU GO TO THE BATHROOM, YOU'LL BE ABLE TO SEE WHETHER YOUR PAD NEEDS CHANGING.

A few dots or swipes of blood are OK to ignore. But if the pad is heavy with blood, it's time to swap a fresh one in.

If you have a physical disability that restricts your movement, you might find pads are the easiest things to use.

You can also buy reusable pads – see page 117 for more information on those.

For my first ever cycle I was changing my pad every one to two hours because I was so conscious of the bleeding. I used up the whole packet of pads! It wasn't until later that I realized a packet was meant to last the whole cycle. There were other women in the house and the pads were supposed to be for all of us, but because I was changing them so regularly I had used them all up! *Hawline. 23*

WHERE DO I PUT USED PADS AND TAMPONS?

Don't flush them down the toilet, as they can block the pipes – instead, wrap them in toilet paper and put them in the nearest bin. You should put their wrappers in the bin, too.

Most women's bathrooms contain sanitary disposal bins for this purpose. If there are no bins anywhere in sight, just wrap your used pad or tampon in toilet paper and tuck it into your bag or pocket to throw out as soon as you see a bin.

Tampons

Tampons absorb period flow from inside the vagina, which involves putting them in (and pulling them out again when they're full). You only use one tampon at a time.

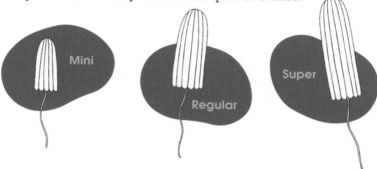

Mini

Regular

Super

Putting your tampon in

First, wash your hands thoroughly, then unwrap the tampon from all the plastic. You'll see a bit of string curled up at one end; loosen it before you insert the tampon.

Then push the tampon up inside your vagina, leaving the string dangling out so you can pull it out later. If it's inserted correctly, the tampon doesn't hurt going in and you can't feel it once it's in there.

Some tampons come with an applicator, which some people find easier to use. Instead of inserting the tampon with your finger, you insert the applicator, which slides the tampon up into your vagina. Then you remove the applicator and throw it away.

Using any kind of tampon means there won't be a bulge in your underwear, which can be good for ballet and gymnastics, and it also means you can go swimming without getting waterlogged.

Taking your tampon out

After three to six hours, wash your hands well and then remove the tampon by finding the string. Then just pull on the string and the tampon should come out easily. If the string isn't dangling down, that's OK – you'll need to feel around until you find it.

Remember to pull down *and* forward, towards your front – if you pull straight down, the tampon can bump against the back wall of the vagina and feel stuck.

The more you use tampons, the easier you'll find it to tell when it's time to change them. A good trick is to tug gently on the string; when the tampon is heavy with blood, it will come out smoothly. If it's still a bit dry, it might be a little stiffer and 'grippy', but it will still come out – or you can leave it in for a little bit longer.

The heavier your flow, the more often you'll need to change your tampon. Different tampons have different absorbency levels, ranging from 'mini' (for light periods) to 'super' (for heavy periods).

TIP

Practising with tampons in between periods or on light period days can be really useful.

TIP

A gentle start can be to practise with mini-tampons, using a bit of lubricant to help the tampon glide in. You can buy lubricant from the supermarket, in the 'personal care' aisle.

It's always interesting to see how much blood the tampon has absorbed. Sometimes a used tampon is dark red and utterly soaked through. Other times it is still mostly white.

On a hectic day, I might use a tampon <u>and</u> a pad at the same time, for the extra level of absorbency – particularly on the first two days of bleeding. *Yumi*

Having trouble?

A common problem is putting the tampon straight up, so that it hits the front wall of the vagina and won't go further. If you tilt the tampon back towards your spine, it will go in easier.

TIP

Our research shows that finding a friend IRL to show you the angle to insert a tampon can make all the difference. You don't have to get nude; they'll just show you over your clothes.

The tampon should go in as far as you can push it (it can't get past your cervix, so you can't possibly lose it), about as far as your second knuckle or, for some, the whole finger-length.

Once it's sitting at the top of the vagina (against the opening of the cervix), you should not be able to feel it inside you when you're walking, running, sitting or lying down. In fact, you might forget it's there! Until it becomes soaked with period blood, and then you might feel a kind of heaviness, or some blood might leak out.

Always remember to free the string of the tampon and have it hanging out when you insert it. If the string isn't dangling down, that's OK – you'll need to feel around until you find it.

LUBE

Using tampons is like learning to ride a bike. It usually takes some practice, but once you get there, it's super easy and you'll never _not_ be able to do it again! Even so, the first few times can be … an experience. Here's what I remember about my early tampon-trouble-times:

"Why doesn't it fit?!"   "Help! Where's the string???"
"Owwww!"   "This is ridiculous! Why is
"Oh no, it's stuck."   it soooo difficult????"

But I kept practising and I figured it out pretty quickly after that! _Dr Melissa_

Get to know your vagina

One of the reasons it can feel weird and difficult to get a tampon in is that you might not be used to feeling the inside of your vagina. A simple tip is to put a clean finger inside your vagina and see how far you can reach up inside. **(It is your body, and you are totally allowed to do this.)** Get to know the inside of your vagina, and how it slopes up towards the chest and back towards the spine. See page 120 for more about the vagina.

Period pants

Period pants are underpants with a cloth pad built in to the crotch area (the bit where your vagina sits). They come in lots of different sizes, absorbencies and styles. The best thing about them is that they can be reused – you just rinse them, put them in the washing machine, and dry them so they're ready for next time!

Period pants are fantastic for people who don't want to use disposable menstrual products. They are also great for people who aren't near shops and can't just pop out for a packet of pads.

Depending on your flow, period pants are great from about day three of your period, when the flow is usually lighter. Using them feels like you don't even have a period! If you have a heavy flow on days one and two, you might like to use them in combination with something else, like a tampon.

If you're still getting used to your period and you're trying period pants for the first time, consider using backup in the form of an extra pad, a tampon or some extra pants over the top.

Period pants can be bought easily online, and are stocked in large department stores. They're more expensive upfront than pads and tampons – prices vary from £10 to around £40 a pair – but they work out much cheaper in the long run.

Tips for using period pants

1. **Rinse them in cold water as soon as you're done with them.** Give them a rinse in the sink or shower as soon as you take them off. It only takes a few seconds, and then they're dealt with immediately. Trust us, you don't want your used period pants drying out and going hard and crusty in the corner of your bedroom!

2. Wash them in cold water.

Once they've been rinsed, they can go in the regular laundry (with other dark or coloured clothes is best) – just make sure it's a cold wash cycle, as heat makes blood congeal.

3. Let them dry. Period pants

take longer to dry than regular pants, so if you want to use them as your main method, you will need at least four to six pairs, and you'll need to wash them regularly.

4. They love sunshine. It's best

to dry them in the sun, not the dryer. If you can't hang them outside, inside is fine – just make sure you give them time to get completely dry before you put them away or use them again.

OTHER USES

Period pants are also popular for people who sweat quite a lot, or who have leaky bladders (this can sometimes happen for people who've had babies). Period pants just wick the moisture away!

Menstrual cups

A menstrual cup is a small silicone cup that you fold over twice and then push up inside your vagina, usually using two fingers. It springs open to its original cup shape once it's inside and catches the blood leaving your uterus.

Menstrual cups are a cheaper and more environmentally friendly way of managing menstruation, as you can reuse them easily – just wash and go! Most chemists sell them, or you can buy them online.

You can use cups for up to 12 hours at a time, making them absolutely magic if you're hopeless at remembering to bring pads to school, or for long trips or work shifts. They're also great if you don't have much money, as one cup – while initially expensive – can last around ten years.

They can be tricky to get the hang of. As with tampons, they take practice, and it's safe to practise in between periods.

The bottom of the cup has a stem just like the stem of a wineglass (without the base). Contrary to popular belief, you do NOT pull on the stem to remove the cup. We'll get to that in a sec!

40–45 mm

45–60 mm

10–20mm

Putting it in

The best way to insert the cup is with a wet cup and dry hands. (The wet cup will slide in more easily and the dry fingers will grip it better.)

1

2

Collapse the cup by flattening it using your fingers, then folding it in half to make it smaller – slightly bigger than a tampon.

collapsed cup

Holding it in this squashed-down shape, insert the cup into your vagina.

3

4

It's handy to remember at this point that it does *not* go in as far as a tampon!

The base of the cup should sit about one centimetre up from the vaginal opening. Do not aim the cup straight up. It should be pointing towards your spine at a 45-degree angle. (If it's too high, it will feel uncomfortable.)

When the cup is in place, allow it to spring open. Many people report that they can feel the 'pop' of it opening. You can adjust it quite easily using your thumb or fingers.

Run your finger around the cup to feel that there are no crunched-up sides. It should be open and smooth, forming a sort of

suction seal around the wall of your vagina. If it's inserted correctly, it shouldn't feel weird or noticeable when you're walking or sitting or doing any other activity. See page 120 for more on the vagina.

TIP

If it seems to be sitting well but there is still some of the stem poking out of your vagina, it means the stem is too long for you. Next time you have it out, use scissors to trim a little length off the end of the stem. (Not too much! You can always cut it back more if you need to.) The cups are designed this way and needing to trim the stem is common.

Taking it out

When removing the cup, it's important to make sure your hands are clean and dry. You might also like to do it over the toilet or in the shower, as a small gush of blood can come out.

First, use the stem as a guide for your fingers to find the top of the cup. Squeeze gently on the cup as close to the rim as possible to break the seal of air that has probably formed. (Squeezing the cup will prevent an air vacuum forming that will make it harder to pull the cup out.) Once you have done this, pull the menstrual cup out. There might be some spillage.

The cup will have filled with menstrual fluid, which you rinse out first in cold water. Then, wash the cup well with warm, soapy water, and rinse again in cold water. Your menstrual cup is ready to reuse.

A menstrual cup that has been collapsed ready for insertion is still bigger than a tampon, so if tampons seem too big and freak you out a bit, you're probably not ready to try a cup yet.

People say to me, "MENSTRUAL CUPS CHANGED MY LIFE!" and "WHY DIDN'T I TRY THESE SOONER?" I love my menstrual cup. I love pulling it out in the shower and getting to see what has come out of my body. It demystifies the whole period process and makes me feel more in tune with my cycle. *Yumi*

KEEPING TRACK OF YOUR PERIOD

To know what's going on with your body, it's really handy to keep track of when you bleed – even though it might take a few months or years for your cycle to become more regular.

You can easily track your period with your school diary or home calendar – start by adding a little red circle on the first day of your flow. (If you have a year-to-a-page in your diary, this could be even easier – then you can see your cycle at a glance.)

The longer you track, the easier you'll find it to predict when your next period might come. You may have heard that a 'monthly' menstrual cycle is 28 days long, but this is just an average – it varies from person to person and can be up to 45 days long for teens. The cycle is counted from the first day of bleeding to the first day of your next period. See page 148 for more on the monthly hormone cycle.

If you like, you can also take note of the length of your period, your moods, discharge and any pain symptoms. Knowing where your grumpy days sit in your cycle can help predict when

My hair gets greasy and I feel super-angry with my dad about four days before. *Max, 13*

I always get a pimple on my chin two or three days before my period is about to start. *Amy, 13*

On the first day of my period, I usually write the letter 'P' (for period) in a big circle on the calendar that we keep on the fridge. And my family draws an angry face on the day when my PMS symptoms are the worst! This helps me predict when my next period will be and when my next grumpy day will be. *Yumi*

your period is coming too. (See page 92 for more on PMS.) If you want to get super-detailed, you can also make notes about cravings, how you sleep, and your energy levels. You might notice lots of changes during this time, or you might notice nothing different at all! It depends on the person.

If you have a smart phone, there is a wide variety of excellent and free apps like **Clue** and **PeriodTracker** that make tracking your period and symptoms easy, and even kind of fun!

The first time came as a surprise. I was 13, turning 14. It was weird – like I didn't really have a cycle – I had it week on, week off for, like, six weeks. And then I had it two weeks off, one week on for about three or four weeks, then it went three weeks off, one week on, four weeks off, one week on, five weeks off, one week on – and it's never really got better. Now it's – I dunno, I get one week in between and it's really light and it just comes out of nowhere and there's no schedule at all! *Kiara, 15*

QUESTIONS FOR DR MELISSA

Discharge!

> **When I went to the toilet the other night, I had all this gooey stuff on my pants. It was clear and white. What is that stuff? Does it mean I am going to get my period?**

Discharge is totally normal and nothing to be alarmed about. As your body develops, the cervix (or the opening of the uterus) is making mucus and the vagina is becoming more moist. This causes a noticeable flow of fluid to come out and end up on your pants. This discharge, or *secretion*, appears as clear or white, and sometimes dries yellow in your pants.

There's no need to freak out about it. This 'goo' is natural, normal and will appear at some point early in puberty. It's just part of your body kicking into gear for menstruation, sex and reproduction. If it bothers you, you can always use a liner to keep the discharge off your pants.

Discharge is a sign everything is going well in

I find it really interesting that no-one ever wants to talk about discharge! Why? It's not discussed much in school sex ed, and a lot of people seem to pretend it doesn't exist! One reason might be because discharge is sometimes connected to sexy feelings. Meaning, sometimes if you're having romantic or sexy thoughts, you'll notice more discharge flow connected to these thoughts (see page 60). It can also just flow for no apparent reason! *Yumi*

your body. The only time you need to worry about it is if it seems to be coming out in copious amounts, has a really strong odour, and/or accompanies itching. A light odour is totally normal. If you think something is wrong with your discharge, go and see your GP or show an older female friend.

There were SO many questions to Dolly Doctor about discharge in the lead-up to the first period! It seemed to freak a lot of people out. It's like everyone is taught, 'OK, here are your boobs, your pubes, and your period. But don't mention the discharge!' *Dr Melissa*

The rest of my body is changing. Does this mean my period is coming?

66 I am 13 but I still don't have my periods. Are there any signs to show me when I am getting them? 99

Doctors and scientists look for a few signs to predict when your period is coming. Developing breasts is the earliest sign, closely followed by pubic hair. It varies, but the first period comes on average two years after your breasts start to develop.

In the months leading up to the first period, you might notice clear fluid coming out of your vagina (the 'secretions', or 'discharge'). Once vaginal secretions become regular over months or even a year or so, it's a good sign that your periods are on their way soon.

Poo It's natural to poo more when you're having a period! During the first couple of days of your period, your body releases a hormone called prostaglandin which does a bunch of things, including getting your uterus to contract to help squeeze out the period blood. (Picture it like an invisible hand squeezing a stress ball.)

This hormone can also work on your intestines, squeezing them and making some of us poo a lot during the first couple of days!

I remember the first time there was a clot – thinking that there was something wrong and not asking anyone about it, just waiting and seeing. I seemed to still be alive a few weeks later, so I figured it was OK! I had never seen anything written about clotting and I didn't know it was a thing. But you can really feel it, particularly when you're wearing a pad. **BLOOD? OF COURSE CLOTTING!**
Amelia, 33

Is a blood clot also my period?

66 **Sometimes during my period I feel like a gush of blood comes out. But when I have a look it turns out to be like a small lump of blood clot. So what is it exactly?** 99

Period blood can be dark red and a thick fluid, or it can be brown and have small bits of tissue (those lining cells) or blood clots. These are nothing to worry about. Your uterus is simply shedding whatever's in there that it doesn't need this time around. Pretty clever, hey?

FACT: The lining of the uterus that sheds (i.e. your period) is a combination of blood, fluid from the cervix and vagina called 'secretions', and special cells from the lining of the uterus. That's why period 'blood' looks different from the blood that you see if, say, you cut your finger.

PERIOD *Challenges*

Handling your period like a boss can take some practice! Here are some common challenges and how you can sail right through them.

What's the worst that can happen?

Once you get your head around the **WORST** that can happen with your period on an ordinary day, you can relax! Because the very worst thing isn't that bad. It won't kill you, or hurt any of the people you care deeply about – it might be a bit embarrassing, but you'll get through it. You might even find it funny when it's over.

Leaks

The worst that can happen is that your period spills out from your underwear and leaks on to your clothes or bedding. Maybe other people will notice,

Yep, it happened to me. So embarrassing. I was 15. I survived. I even laughed about it later. *Dr Melissa* maybe not. Maybe you'll feel mortified, but you'll put in a fresh pad, tie a jumper around your waist, and get on with life.

If you're unlucky, you might bleed on to the car upholstery, the bus seat, your wheelchair, or someone's couch. If that happens, you'll do your best to wipe it off and maybe you'll feel bad for a short time – but it's not a big deal. It might even seem funny.

If you're caught out with a leak, stay calm. Depending on where you are, you might feel OK to just casually get up and find a bathroom where you can deal with the leak. Leaks on to dark clothes or thicker fabrics, like denim, aren't going to be so obvious. In fact, they may not be noticeable at all. You might be able to wait until you get home to sort it out. It might be a small enough leak that you can sponge it off with cold water.

If you're nowhere near a bathroom or if you're wearing light-coloured clothes, your best bet is to put something around your bum. If necessary, call for help. A friend, your mum or sister – anyone nearby who can lend you their jacket to tie around your waist. Jumpers, bags, scarves and spare clothing can also work. Challenges like this can make us very creative!

My mum was really nurturing and taught me how to wrap up a used pad and throw it out properly. I remember asking her if she was grossed out by interacting with my used pad. And she was like, "No, it's so normal! It's not dirty or gross." She said she was my mum and so she wasn't grossed out by my pads. She had it all neatly wrapped and said, "It's fine now, you can just throw it in the bin." *Marihuzka, 36*

Smells

Because your pad is close to your body and warm from your body heat, you may be able to smell it when you go to the bathroom and take down your underpants. But don't fret about other people smelling it the rest of the time. When the pad is locked away inside your underwear, there isn't such a strong odour – and everyone else is further away from the source than you!

Even so, the worst that can happen is that you forget to shower one day, and have a bit of a period odour that other people can smell. So you'll go home and have a shower. No big deal.

> In all my life, I have never smelled anyone's period blood but my own. *Yumi* (who has an excellent sense of smell)

TO MANAGE SMELLS, CHANGE YOUR UNDERWEAR EVERY DAY, AND SHOWER ONCE A DAY AND YOU SHOULD BE FINE.

Having your period is nothing to be ashamed about. Neither is carrying pads or tampons or your period pack. So you shouldn't be ashamed if a pad or tampon falls out of your bag in front of other people. Either ignore it, or put it back in your bag, or put it in the bin – easy!

All that will happen is that other people will know that you get your period sometimes, and so what? So does half the population.

PART OF GROWING UP IS PERFECTING YOUR SHRUG.

Stuck

What if a tampon gets stuck and you can't get it out?

First up, don't stress out – this has happened to people before, so you're not the only one!

Now, let me reassure you: a tampon **cannot get lost** in your vagina – it has nowhere to go but out, so eventually it WILL come out, one way or another.

The best thing to do is wash your hands, and then insert a clean finger (or two fingers) to try to pull it out yourself. Take the time to do it calmly in a place where you feel safe. The shower or toilet, for instance, where you know you probably won't be interrupted, and where you can safely try. Don't use any other tools to try to get it out – this could be dangerous.

If you've tried your best to get the tampon out and you definitely can't, you will have to go to your doctor, or a Family Planning Clinic if there's one nearby, where a doctor or nurse will be able to get it out. Yes, it will be embarrassing, but don't worry – everyone who works in these places has seen a thousand bums and vaginas and they're fantastically unshockable. You can ask for a female practitioner if you prefer. (For more on stuck tampons, see 'Is There Something Wrong?' page 126).

FACT

The WORST THING THAT COULD POSSIBLY HAPPEN … has already happened to someone before … and they survived it. And you will too!

69

PERIOD
Challenges

At school

To be honest, you are very likely to get your period at least some of the time at school. The good news is that **YOU CAN MANAGE IT!** It's not impossible. The bad news is that managing your period at school can take some energy.

You have to:

⭐ **Think ahead** and plan for your period. Keep your period pack in your schoolbag at all times! See page 20 for what should go in it.

⭐ **Anticipate your period days.** If you know it's coming (and let's face it, it's coming sooner or later), be prepared with extra pads or tampons. See page 58 for more info on tracking your cycle.

⭐ **Check in on your pad or tampon** when you've got your period. Check it at break and lunch *before* you hang out with your friends. That way, you won't worry about whether you're leaking – trust us, it's worth it!

Whether you let your friends know or keep your period to yourself, here's what else you need to know to handle it like a boss.

If you feel comfortable, consider telling your friends that you have your period. I used to be really secretive about it, but then I realized that chances are at least one person is going through the same thing. You can be chocolate-and-bathroom-buddies! *Yumi*

Bring your supplies

Pack a couple more pads or tampons than you think you'll need, just in case. If your schoolbag has a side pocket, you can put them in there, or just keep your period pack topped up every day.

If you have pockets, you can put two or three pads/tampons in your pocket in the morning before you leave the house and know that you're set for the whole day. If you have a locker, why not leave a whole packet in there for when you need it?

Change your pad or tampon at break and lunchtime, before sport and, if it's a long trip home, after school as well.

You'll want me later!

On school days I make sure I pack all my pads in the morning. You need at least three big pads per day and a tampon. And some chocolate. *Lisa, 15*

Know your bathrooms

Suss out which toilet cubicles at your school have bins or sanitary disposal units, and get in the habit of using those particular cubicles once in a while, even before you get your period.

If you're at primary school, you might discover that the bathrooms don't have sanitary bins in the toilet cubicles – which is annoying. There is always a bin in the actual bathroom itself, but there are often none in the stalls, meaning you have to wrap up your used pad or tampon in toilet paper, take it out of the cubicle, and place it in the communal rubbish bin.

This is not a big deal, but it's also not great. You deserve a bin that you can use in the privacy of the toilet cubicle. I recommend you ask your most kick-ass parent (or friend's parent) to speak to the school and ask that bins be installed in at least one of the toilet cubicles. Or, if you're comfortable, go direct – figure out which teacher has the power to create change in your school and explain your situation.

Assert yourself if you need to check in during class

Sometimes you need to change a pad or tampon during class time, although naturally your teachers would prefer you took care of it during lunch and break! Still, it's OK if you need to go – just politely ask permission to go to the bathroom. If they say no, it's perfectly fine to go up to them and say, "I have my period and I'm going to bleed all over the place if you don't let me go to the toilet."

Pain at school

Feeling gross? It's all right to take a small amount of paracetamol or ibuprofen to help you get through. (There's more info on pain management on page 96.) You can also pack foods that make you feel good on these days – ginger helps with bloating and nausea, and celery might make you feel bouncy instead of sluggish. And a bit of dark chocolate can always brighten your period days.

If you feel really unwell, you can go to sick bay for a quick lie-down. But try to avoid throwing a sickie and going (or staying) home, unless the pain or the bleeding is actually unmanageable. Bailing on class disadvantages you, as you need ALL your learning to become your most awesome self.

PERIOD
Challenges

Playing sport

You can totally handle being active while you have your period. If you change into a uniform to play sport, this is a good opportunity to swap in a fresh pad or tampon to see you through the game or lesson. Tampons are a good option if you are running around a lot, as they are invisible – and you won't feel them at all.

Choose sports shorts that make you feel the most supported – dark colours are good, and a snug fit that makes you feel all tucked in is also good. Some girls like to wear a version of bike shorts or leggings underneath their uniform shorts, or an extra pair of pants to keep everything secure.

Did you know that exercise can help you feel good when you've got your period? It's actually a recommended way to manage period pain! Exercise releases natural endorphins, which are chemicals that make us feel good. It's a super-helpful tool on your PMS days for this reason, too.

Just remember that running around will make you sweaty, and it's common to mistake the feeling of being sweaty down below for the feeling of blood leaking out. If you've just changed your pad, this is very unlikely! But if you want to check, you can always go to the bathroom halfway through.

Depending on your relationship with your sports teacher, you might even be able to tell them at the start of the lesson, "I just got my period and would really like to be able to go to the bathroom halfway through, if that's OK." Teachers, let me tell you, LOVE this kind of communication. It makes them feel respected and it totally stimulates their kindness glands.

If your period is making you feel really unwell or sore, you can also let your teacher know that you need to sit out your game or lesson.

Some people say that having your period is like a big red button. You just press it and the teachers will let you skip sport!

But because of this goodwill, we think it's important not to abuse it – only skip sport if you really feel you can't handle it.

PERIOD *Challenges*

Swimming days

If you can wear a tampon or a menstrual cup, you can go swimming without having to worry about blood. Just change your tampon before you get into the pool (or when you change into your swimming costume) and you'll be fine. See page 46 for info on how to use a tampon or page 54 for how to use a menstrual cup. Ordinary sanitary pads are no good for swimming as they will absorb water instead of blood. Water can also stop the adhesive glue on pads from working.

If tampons aren't an option for you right now, period swimwear (which hold special pads in place while you swim) are a thing, just like period pants. They aren't super common, though, and need to be ordered online.

At school camp I had no idea about periods, so I just put a pad in my swimmers and went for a swim! I thought you could do that! Lucky nobody noticed because I reckon that would've stuck – you know, I would've been the Period Swimmers Kid. I remember thinking, 'This doesn't actually feel right.' It got all waterlogged and heavy – actually, it felt like a massive poo in your pants! **NOT GOOD AT ALL.** *Gracie, 37*

For when you really can't swim

If you're not up to tampons yet, that's OK. No-one can force you to use them. We have heard of a few instances of teachers insisting you should use a tampon and take the swimming lesson and, frankly, that's not on. Involve a carer or parent if you need backup.

If you're worried about pushback from teachers, the first step is to ask your parent or carer to write a note for you to explain the situation. Here's a template:

> Dear Teacher,
>
> Please excuse *First Name Last Name* from school swimming today and tomorrow. She has her period and would prefer to sit it out.
>
> Thank you for your understanding.
>
> Sincerely,
> *Parent Name*

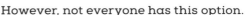

However, not everyone has this option.

My mum and dad had jobs that meant they worked like crazy, so getting either one of them to write a note for school was a big deal. I mostly avoided it, and managed a lot of my own school stuff. *Yumi*

If, like Yumi, you have parents who aren't that involved in the day-to-day management of your school life, you may have to manage the situation yourself. Here are some ways to explain why you can't swim. Some are true and some are a bit bendy with the truth. We always think it's better to be honest, but you'll know better than anyone what will work for your situation:

Swimming days I can usually survive with a tampon and one really thin pad that I wear into the pool. Before I knew how to use tampons I just wouldn't swim.
Anouk, 15

I can't swim today because I have my period.

I can't swim today because I don't want to.

My mum says I can't swim because I've had a cold for the past week.

My doctor says I shouldn't swim for another week because I'm still a bit fluey.

Please don't make me swim today because I absolutely do not want to have to explain to you that I have my period.

I want to swim but I can't because I've had gastro.

Our advice to you is: always approach the teacher respectfully *and* early. So if swimming or sport is in the afternoon, have a word to them in the morning so that they know what's coming. Teachers love a bit of a warning and appreciate you showing that you're not ignoring sport, or that you haven't forgotten your gear, or that you aren't just being lazy.

This is another good reason to only pull the 'period card' when you absolutely need to. If you do it all the time, it may not work when you really need it!

My school won't let me skip sport!

If your school has super-strict rules about missing sport or swimming and insists on a note from a doctor, then you could:

 Get a note from your doctor that will cover you, about once a month, for the whole year.

 Get your parent or carer on board to question rules about needing a doctor to confirm you have periods … um, duh …

 BRING IT ON: talk with friends, other students, your favourite teacher and/or the headteacher about getting the school rules changed, since menstruation should not be something that students need to get a doctor's certificate for. It's a natural part of life, not an illness!

PERIOD *Challenges*

Sleepovers

If you don't feel up to going to a sleepover when you've got your period, you don't have to go. But, really, there's no reason to miss out on overnight fun with your friends!

The easiest way to handle having your period during a sleepover is to tell your friend(s). It's not a big deal, and people get their periods all the time. This way, when you take your period pack to the bathroom to check in, it doesn't need to feel like a secret.

Remember that when you change your pad or tampon at a friend's house, it's a good idea to wrap up the used one in toilet paper and put it in the bin (not the toilet) – just like you'd do at home. If there's no bin in their bathroom, just wrap it up and put it in the nearest one.

If you don't want to tell anyone at the sleepover that you have your period, you totally don't have to. You'll just need to be organized with your supply of pads, as finding the toilet at night and managing sanitary supplies in a strange house may be tricky!

YOU MIGHT LIKE TO PUT YOUR PERIOD PACK SOMEWHERE EASY TO FIND IN THE DARK, OR STASH A COUPLE OF PADS INSIDE THE BATHROOM BEFORE IT GETS TO SLEEP TIME.

Springing a leak at a sleepover

Even though it seems a bit 'worst-case scenario', it's totally common for people to leak on to the bedsheets or sleeping bag when they're staying at a friend's house. It's not the end of the world and nobody is going to hate you for doing this.

EEK!

Don't even worry about it! 😊

If it happens, tell your friend what has happened, or tell your friend's parent. Most people are pretty understanding. They will just change and wash the sheets, and life will go on.

Reinforcements

If your flow is heavy or you're worried about spillage, here are some extra precautions you can take:

⭐ **'Overnight' pads** are extra absorbent and can take a lot of liquid before they start to spill over. Swap out your regular pad for an overnight one right before bedtime.

⭐ **A tampon as well as a pad** is a pretty good way to keep a regular flow under control. (If the tampon leaks, it'll leak into the pad – pretty clever, huh?) Put the tampon in last thing at night and you might find it lasts right through until morning anyway.

> At night I used to have a lot of accidents. They didn't really have overnight pads then and you'd wake up in the night thinking everything was all right, but then it'd be a bloodbath because you'd leaked out the back of your pad! To fix this, I would layer a whole bunch of toilet paper and renovate the pad, adding a whole toilet paper extension to the butt-crack area. *Audrey, 37*

⭐ If you're not up to tampons, **try wearing a pad with another pair of pants over the top** to keep it firmly in place. You could even wear period pants over your regular pad to add an extra layer of protection.

⭐ **Thick, dark tracksuit pants worn as pyjamas**, or just some decent dark pyjamas, will add another layer of protection.

⭐ Finally, it is perfectly OK and common to **sleep with a towel under your hips**. Bring one from home if you want to be super-prepared.

> One time I had a sleepover at a male friend's house and I got my period. The boys were swimming in the backyard pool the whole time and I couldn't tell them the truth, so they kept saying, 'Get in, Anouk! Get in!' All night I was worried that I would leak while I was asleep! It was hellish. I ended up using toilet paper for pads overnight and it was actually fine. Hellish, but fine. *Anouk, 15*

PERIOD Challenges

Camping

You don't have to miss out on camping just because you've got your period!

Just as campers have to organize food, water and clothes, you'll need to plan ahead with your supplies. And even if you don't expect to get your period on your next hike or camping adventure, it's worth packing some supplies anyway. Getting caught out is annoying.

There are a few factors that arise while camping that you don't even have to *think* about in the modern world:

1 It will probably be harder to get to running water to wash your hands and shower when you're camping.

2 If you forget some key supplies, it'll be much harder to duck to the shops to stock up.

(3) **You're not usually doing the laundry when you're camping, so you need to make sure you've got more than enough clean clothes and underwear to stay feeling fresh or to manage if there's a spill.**

(4) **Disposing of rubbish might be something you only get to do at the end of the holiday, meaning you'll have to keep it all stored in a bag somewhere – like in your tent or backpack.**

It's a good idea to organize a **special camping period pack**, which is much like a regular period pack with a few additions. It should contain:

 ⭐ **Enough pads and tampons** for each day of your period. So if you usually bleed for four days and use five pads a day, you will need 20 pads. Plus a few spares.

⭐ **Extra pants and swimmers,** in case of leakage (and also because sometimes it's just nice to have a fresh pair to change into).

☆ **Hand sanitiser and/or baby wipes.** You don't need to be germ-phobic to want clean hands! It is GREAT to have the option to clean your hands when there's no water and soap available, especially before putting in or taking out a tampon or going to the toilet. Hand sanitiser comes in small travel-sized bottles.

☆ **Three large plastic bags.** Ziplock bags are great, because nothing inside is going to spill out, including smells. The first bag is for all your rubbish to go into (which you could label clearly as 'RUBBISH' if you LOVE being super-organized like Yumi does). The second bag is for dirty pants (which Yumi would gleefully label 'DIRTY PANTS'). And the third bag is a spare, in case you have the opportunity to throw out the rubbish bag halfway through your period and can start a fresh one.

☆ **One entire set of fresh clothes.** Pack things that aren't your favourites into a separate bag, so you won't miss them while they're stashed away. That way, if you leak on to your clothes, or are even just feeling crusty and gross, you've got a glorious clean set of clothes! It's like a little present from your past self!

PERIOD
Challenges

I live with my dad

Parent management

Here's the thing: for most kids, there's an element of having to manage your parents or carers, whether it's a mum, a dad, a foster-carer, grandparent or someone else. The people who care for you can't know all your preferences or everything you need. So you have to keep communicating what suits and doesn't suit, what you like and don't like, and what's going on in your life so that your carer can help.

Some carers are better at listening to this kind of communication than others! And some might not even need to be told. For instance, some parents might automatically know to stock up on period stuff without having to be asked. Others will need to be asked and then maybe reminded several times.

Dads are no different. Some will be super-thoughtful, think of your needs, plan ahead and be awesome, and some will forget and just need a little more 'parent management'. The main difference is that most dads haven't had their periods their whole lives like most mums have. Keep that in mind if you live with your dad.

SOME WAYS TO MANAGE DAD
(OR THE PERSON WHO IS HELPING YOU)

1. **Organize a monthly allowance** where your dad gives you, say, £10 that is just for you to buy period supplies.

2. **Have a dedicated spot** where period supplies sit. Teach your dad to notice when they're running low, and to stock up next time he's at the shops.

3. **Text your dad** when you need him to get you some pads or tampons. If possible, include a photo of your preferred brand so he gets the right ones.

4. **There are these awesome online 'period subscription' services,** where your supplies arrive in the mail every month, like magic! Get your dad's support in finding an online period subscription where you receive your preferred supplies in the post. The money comes off his card, the boxes go to you.

5. **Give him a copy of this book** for his next birthday, Father's Day or as a random present. Point out this page and ask him which way he wants to be managed. Also encourage him to read the whole book. (Hi Dad! *waves*) He will learn a lot about periods and that's a good thing.

⭐ **Empty the bathroom bins yourself.** This isn't much fun, but neither is an overflowing bin.

⭐ **Keep supplies** of ibuprofen and paracetamol around the house, in the car and in your schoolbag.

⭐ **Change your own sheets** and get the washed ones dried and put away (or even do the laundry yourself). This is a bit boring, but it's worth it for the delightful clean-sheets feeling.

⭐ **Stay on top of your fresh pants situation.** Do your laundry, and pipe up when you need to buy more!

PERIOD *Challenges*

Emergency measures

EVERYONE has been caught out getting their period when they have **NO STUFF** – no period pack, no regular supplies in the bathroom cupboard, no emergency stash. Nothing. This happens to everyone – **EVERYONE** – so chances are it'll happen to you. If there's one thing that getting your period teaches you, it's the lifelong skill of **RESOURCEFULNESS**. You can:

 Ask your friends or other people in the women's bathrooms whether they have any spare supplies you could have. You'd be surprised at how often this works! For instance, you could say, 'Excuse me, do you happen to have a spare pad or tampon, please?'

Check at the front desk – many workplaces have a first aid kit that contains pads. This includes schools, hospitals and sports clubs, and they are usually pretty happy to hand them over.

Use a little brother or sister's **nappy**. If you're desperate!

 Fold up some **toilet paper** and use it to line your pants. It will work for a short amount of time and, luckily, toilet paper tends to be in generous supply in most toilets. If you're stuck for a few hours, you might need to check in on it every hour or so.

 Our school is pretty cool. Any time you want, you can go to Student Reception and you just have to say "That time of the month" and they'll give you some pads. *Lisa, 15*

 Use **spare socks** ... but wet wool makes me itch!

 Use a mini-pack of **travel tissues**. The perfect shape!

 Use a small **flannel or hand towel**, which you can wash when you get home.

To help out your future self, you can also make sure you have emergency supplies stashed in a pocket of every bag you own, the glovebox of the family car, and your musical instrument case, just in case. Even just one pad or tampon could save you down the track.

I once went into a chemist without any money and asked if I could have some pads and pay them back later. They said yes. I remembered to pay them back, OF COURSE, because WHO COULD FORGET?! *Yumi*

WHAT TO DO IF YOU FEEL RUBBISH

There are lots of reasons to feel special about getting your period: you're growing up, your body is changing, and nature is cool. But sometimes you might feel a bit rubbish – teary, grumpy, shouty, quiet – and that's normal!

Why am I so grumpy? Is PMS even real?

Yes, it is definitely real.

PMS stands for 'premenstrual syndrome'. It's a collection of symptoms that happen during a very specific time in the menstrual cycle – between ovulation and when your period arrives. PMS symptoms STOP once bleeding starts. (To get a clear picture of where PMS lands in the cycle, see page 58, but basically it's a few days before you bleed.)

The main symptoms of PMS include:

- ✰ irritability
- ✰ mood swings
- ✰ anxiety
- ✰ depression
- ✰ swelling
- ✰ bloating
- ✰ breast tenderness
- ✰ headaches

It doesn't affect everyone, but it can be a problem for up to 30 per cent of teens. Those with moderate to severe period pain are more likely to also have PMS.

Treatments

Despite so many teenagers and older women having PMS, the cause is still not fully understood – although it is related to period hormone patterns in some way. And while it is definitely real, it shouldn't be used as an excuse to treat others badly. You'd be surprised to know how many grown women, who've been bleeding for years, honestly believe they're just cranky and don't realize they've been experiencing PMS until the PMS is over. Every month!

There are effective ways to treat PMS symptoms:

The Pill

Because PMS is related to fluctuating menstrual cycle hormones, actually using some hormones can help with symptoms. The most useful of these can be found in contraceptive pills, which can be used in the 'usual' way – in other words, taking them every day, or taking them just during the second phase of the menstrual cycle. It's best to talk to a doctor first to figure out what your specific needs are.

Antidepressants

Low doses of some antidepressant medication also work for some people, since mood changes seem to result from the interaction between menstrual hormones and brain chemicals.

Counselling

Similarly, a certain type of counselling technique used for treating depression – called cognitive behaviour therapy – can work. Talk to your doctor to learn more.

Over-the-counter supplements

Calcium supplements can be effective for some PMS symptoms. Some people find that agnus castus extract helps, and in the past Vitamin B6 and evening primrose oil have been used, but there is less evidence that these work.

Before my period, I feel like crying

You know what? It's totally OK to just feel your feelings.

Remember that the emotions will pass – especially once you start to bleed. It can make you feel better to have a cry – ring a friend, sit with a parent or have some 'you' time with an emotional movie or a favourite book. Plenty of brave, fierce and awesome people have needed to snuggle up with a hot water bottle and chocolate and just spend some time feeling rubbish in order to feel better.

Personally, I like to do a boxing class and just punch it out. *Yumi*

Eating well can help PMS too

PMS can cause a feeling of bloating and cravings for junk food! But trust us: excessive sugar (like lollies), salt (like crisps) and caffeine (like soft drink) are really **NO HELP**, before your period or when you're bleeding and already feeling a bit gross in your body.

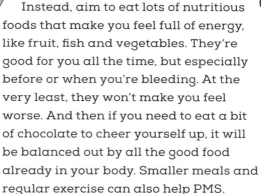

Instead, aim to eat lots of nutritious foods that make you feel full of energy, like fruit, fish and vegetables. They're good for you all the time, but especially before or when you're bleeding. At the very least, they won't make you feel worse. And then if you need to eat a bit of chocolate to cheer yourself up, it will be balanced out by all the good food already in your body. Smaller meals and regular exercise can also help PMS.

My period usually drains out most of my energy. The great thing about my first period was I stayed home with Mum. We went out for breakfast, which was really nice. I told my friends I had got my period and they were like, "Oh my gosh do you know how awful this is?! Do you have a headache? Do you have stomach pain?" And I was like, "It's not that bad!", except the next day I was like, "You were right, it is that bad!" *Tans. 13*

HOW TO HANDLE PERIOD PAIN

Most people don't get any period pain for six to twelve months after their first period, but then it becomes fairly common. Very common, actually – 75 per cent or more of teenagers will experience mild or moderate period pain, and 10 per cent or so may get severe pain.

It's not all bad, though!

Fast facts:

⭐ **Most period pain lasts for one to two days only.**

⭐ **Period pain treatments are very effective in most cases.**

⭐ **If the simple treatments don't work, there are other options.**

I know this sounds grim, but most of us with mild period pain get used to it ... and it becomes just a bit of background noise. *Yumi*

What causes the period pain?

As the lining of the uterus begins to shed at the beginning of your period, the cells in this lining release a hormone called prostaglandin. This prostaglandin helps the muscular wall of the uterus contract, which squeezes out the lining more effectively. Sometimes there's a bit of overkill – too much prostaglandin, too much muscle contraction – and it goes into a sort of cramp.

In people with bad period pain, levels of prostaglandin can generally be higher. The prostaglandin from the uterus can also cause other physical effects like nausea, vomiting, bloating and headaches.

Prostaglandin also causes your intestines to wake up and get active – so it's common to poo more at the beginning of your period!

I was really young – just 10 years old – and nobody else in my school had it. I remember just feeling really sick at school and having really, really bad pain. When I got home, I realized that I had it. The next day all the other kids were like, "Are you OK?" And I was like, "Yeah, I got my period." Because I was the first person BY FAR to get my period, everyone was super interested! I think a lot of friends thought it would actually hurt having the blood coming out, so I was able to explain that it was just the feeling sick leading up to your period, and that the pain was kind of in your body (not in your vagina). *Nadine, 35*

Some people find just one of these treatments works, while others use a combination. Experiment and find out what works for you!

Period pain tablets

Ibuprofen

These are the most effective tablets for period pain that you can buy at the supermarket, or over the counter at the chemist (you don't need a prescription for them). Ibuprofen can have lots of different names, so look for the word 'ibuprofen' in the small print – that is the actual name of the active ingredient. They're also known as non-steroidal anti-inflammatories. These tablets work best if they are taken as soon as your period starts, before the pain hits. That's because they counteract the release of the prostaglandin hormones in the uterus that cause cramping and other symptoms such as nausea, bloating and headaches. Taking non-steroidal anti-inflammatory tablets according to the instructions on the packet can help all of these symptoms. And if one brand doesn't work, try a different one next time (not on the same day!).

Remember to always stick to the recommended dosage for painkillers, and check with your parent or carer before you take anything!

Paracetamol

Paracetamol is a commonly used painkiller, often taken for headaches. It's effective for period pain, though not usually quite as effective as ibuprofen.

These tablets can have side effects too, as with any medication. But in general the benefit of period pain relief outweighs the side effects.

Heat Lying down with a heat pack or hot water bottle over your lower tummy or lower back can help. Combining this with your favourite movie and some occasional loud complaining can enhance the soothing effect … although this has not been scientifically proven!

Exercise It sounds crazy, but exercise really helps period pain! Sometimes going for a run or doing something very physically active – like a fitness class, swimming or cycling – really helps. It can get your circulation going and make you feel happier, plus distract you from the discomfort.

Relaxation

'Relaxation' does not mean blobbing around eating junk food! We're talking about relaxation techniques such as breathing exercises, meditation and visualisations.

These techniques can take some practice, but are great for managing pain in the rest of your life, too.

Vitamin B1 and fish oil supplements

These don't necessarily work as a treatment WHEN you get your period. But some research is showing that taking 100mg of vitamin B1 a day can reduce period pain over time. It's possible that fish oil supplements can help in this way too. Fish oil supplements contain omega-3 fatty acids, which you also get from food. Oily fish are the best sources of omega-3 fatty acids, and plant-based sources include flaxseed, soybeans, walnuts and wild rice.

Other vitamins and supplements

Magnesium supplements seem to be beneficial for period pain. Some studies have looked at calcium, zinc, vitamin E, vitamin D and ginger powder and found that they might help.

Chinese medicine and acupuncture

Chinese medicine can help period pain, and seems to be more effective than acupuncture.

CAN I MAKE MY PERIODS STOP?

Is it possible to suppress your period? Can you do it for a long time? The answer is **yes**.

There might be a medical or health-related reason for stopping periods. Or you might decide after a few months or years of having monthly bleeds that you'd like to reduce their frequency or intensity.

People with very heavy or painful periods or bad PMS (see page 92) can really benefit from medical treatments that make periods lighter or less painful. This might also mean less time off school, not having to skip sport and not having to miss fun. (See 'Is Something Wrong?' page 126). Another scenario is periods causing distress because of gender identity. (See page 106.)

For some people, there isn't a specific health reason for stopping periods. Some might want to stop them short-term because of travel, a special event or some other convenience-related issue. Others are happy to take a holiday from periods for months, or years.

When I first started getting my period, this would have been the first chapter I'd have turned to. *Yumi*

MYTH BUSTER

Some people worry that it's not safe to stop yourself from bleeding regularly. Back in the days before there was any really effective contraception, many women spent a lot of their lives pregnant or breastfeeding frequently. Both these situations cause periods to stop, and many women would go for years without a period. It wasn't harmful to skip your period then, and it isn't harmful to do it now, either.

Today, for whatever reason, people can also choose to stop or reduce the frequency of periods by using medications or treatments that need a doctor's prescription. While it's important to discuss any prescription medication with your doctor to make sure it's safe for you, the actual fact of not bleeding is generally safe.

The Pill

The simplest way to suppress menstruation is to take hormonal contraception. The one that's been around the longest is 'the Pill'. Getting the Pill involves a visit to the doctor, a check-up and, if all good, a prescription. This is a tried and tested, safe and very effective treatment for period pain. The Pill was designed as a contraceptive (in other words, to prevent pregnancy), but many people take it just for period pain.

The way it works is that it contains hormones that mimic some of the natural period hormones.

THE PILL

The Pill hormones 'talk' to the ovaries (telling them not to ovulate) and to the uterus (telling it not to prepare a thick lining this month).

A cycle of the Pill usually involves taking 28 daily tablets – 21 hormone pills, plus seven sugar pills that don't actually do anything. Taking the sugar pills means your body has a break from the Pill hormones. For most people, this sugar-pill week causes your body to have a hormone-withdrawal bleed, which is similar to a regular menstrual bleed, but lighter and less painful. It's lighter and less painful because the Pill hormones have slowed down the usual build-up of uterine lining.

If you keep taking the hormone pills instead of the sugar pills over those seven days, you stop your body from having the hormone-withdrawal bleed.

Meaning, simply: you don't have a bleed.

Many people on the Pill choose to take the hormone pills continuously – maybe for three months, maybe for a year. It's not a total guarantee that you won't bleed at all during this time – something called 'break-through bleeding' can happen, and just means you have a light, period-like bleed while taking the hormone pills.

These effects on your period cycle are temporary – they only last as long as you take the Pill. When you stop, your cycle returns to its natural state.

I once made it to the finals of a diving competition (!) and I didn't know how to use a tampon. I didn't want to miss out, so I organized the Pill with my doctor. *Yumi*

Other hormonal contraceptive methods

As well as the Pill, there are other more involved hormonal methods that can stop you from getting your period. One is the contraceptive implant, or 'rod', that is inserted into your arm by a doctor.

Another is the hormone IUD (intrauterine device). Getting it involves a simple procedure where you take off your pants, lie down on a bed, and have a doctor find their way up inside your vagina using an instrument called a speculum. The doctor then puts a small, T-shaped device inside the uterus, which releases the hormone slowly over five years. It's a really good treatment for heavy menstrual bleeding.

hormone reservoir

flexible arms

Taking any of these hormone contraceptive methods is not a guarantee that periods will skip or stop. You should talk to your doctor first about whether any of these options would work for you, and what the risks are. Some people will still experience irregular or ongoing bleeding while using these methods.

It might be worth having a chat with family members to see what has worked for them, whether there were any side effects, and whether they experienced anything negative from using these methods.

Society expects things of my body that aren't right for me

A small percentage of people find that the body they are born with makes other people expect them to be a 'girl' or a 'boy', but that this is not how they *themselves* feel about their gender. Those who are assigned female at birth might grow up feeling that they identify as boys (or vice versa), or they might just be unsure. They might have done lots of things since childhood to make themselves feel and appear more like boys, such as the way they dressed and the activities and hobbies they chose. The umbrella term for this is 'transgender', or just 'trans'.

As puberty approaches, the idea of getting a period can therefore be *beyond* scary – it can be the worst thing imaginable. But it totally depends on the person – even if they don't feel fully like a girl, the idea of a period might be OK. The trans identity may be something that comes later.

Transgender children, adolescents and adults have existed for as long as time. Just as we now have the medical technology to help girls and women manage their periods, doctors can also help transgender adolescents who don't want to have any periods. We can try to reduce the psychological distress that periods can cause by using hormones to try to block or stop them from coming.

Fortunately, there is a lot more understanding now of transgender people and their rights and needs. If this feels familiar to you, the best option is to speak to a parent or carer, as well as your doctor or an adult you trust.

There are some good websites with information as well – your doctor can direct you to the most relevant ones.

I was pretty fortunate because my periods stopped a month or so after I started taking testosterone. I was presenting as male for a long while before I started taking it. Because of my dysphoria, my own brain made it feel disastrous to have to go and buy tampons. But now, not so much. I have a beard, and I rarely get misgendered. Recently my testosterone dipped and I got a bleed, and I just went to the chemist and bought tampons. I said to the shop assistant, "Where are your sanitary items?" and she said, "You mean, female hygiene products?" and I said, "No. I mean sanitary items." *Nevo, 22*

HYGIENE AND YOUR PERIOD

There is no law dictating what should and shouldn't happen during your period, and that includes showering and managing your hygiene. If you want to go your own way with this, that's totally OK. We're writing this chapter a bit like we're talking to our own kids – meaning, this reflects our own preferences and cultures.

So. What would we advise our kids to do?

Have a shower every day

If you've been a bit slack about daily showers before puberty, now that you're getting your period, it's a good time to start being more disciplined. Your skin and hair tends to get dirty or oily more quickly now, and we'd rather you weren't dirty or smelly.

Showering is the perfect time to refresh. Take out your tampon, throw away your pad, hop in the shower and give your vulva and vagina a good rinse with water.

Once you finish your shower, dry off and put in a new pad or tampon and fresh knickers. Period blood is not dirty or gross, but it does have a colour and if it sticks around long enough, it can give off a smell – kind of like a rusty odour. Showering regularly is a good way to make sure you feel sprightly and clean. You might also like to use dark-coloured towels, to hide any little period stains that might appear when you dry between your legs.

SOAP AND YOUR VULVA

Water or a plain, unscented soap is the best thing to use for your vulva, around your anus and perineum – in other words, all the outside bits. You do NOT need to get soap up inside the vagina. Avoid wipes, gels, deodorants and douches as these can irritate the skin and kill the helpful bacteria that live inside your vagina.

Wash your hands!

Around your regular toileting, you should be washing your hands with soap. Take extra care to remember to do this on days when you've got your period. The best practice is to wash your hands before you go in to the toilet to change your pad or tampon. Then wash your hands again thoroughly afterwards.

There have been lots of people in my life who have quite good showering hygiene, but then would hop out of their towel and put on the same clothes they were wearing before. Which is fine if the clothes don't have a big old tang of BO and sweat and ass through them. Try to keep your clothes clean, and mind the smells that can come from armpits and unwashed bras as well. *Yumi*

WHAT DO BOYS THINK OF PERIODS?

Who cares?

Just joking.
(SORT OF.)

What boys think about periods isn't something you can control – so it really doesn't matter what they think. But if your friends are boys, of course it matters. Your brother, your boyfriend, your sports mates, your dad – they all matter loads. You want them to understand this important part of your life.

If you're pretty new to periods, chances are the boys in your life will still be learning, too. Most boys usually end up being pretty cool and supportive and respectful around periods, but it can take a few goes before they get there. Partly because of the age they're at, and partly because they probably haven't been exposed to as many frank and honest conversations about periods as you have. And partly because they'll never have to actually go through it the way you will.

Just like you care what your guy friends or brothers are going through in their lives, it matters that they care about what you're going through in yours. So talk to them about it in a matter-of-fact way. Answer their questions if you feel like it, or else you could lend them this book. The 'Being an Ally' section on page 112 is a good place for them to start.

But remember, you're the one who's most affected by your period – not them. So let them follow your lead.

And unless they plan on moving to a world without women, all the boys you know now will – for the rest of their lives – have to deal with people who'll have periods. Understanding periods can only be a good thing for them, right now and into the future.

When little brothers or male classmates act all spun-out and horrified by periods, it's pretty annoying. We're not a horror show just because we bleed. I think it's at this time in our development it really hits home that boys just don't mature as fast as the rest of us. *Yumi*

I got my period in Year Seven. Me and my friends have a code word for periods so you can help each other out and lend each other pads and stuff. Our code word is "Guys, guys, guys, guys!" But now we're at high school everyone is really comfortable talking about periods. *Dee Dee, 13*

BEING AN ALLY

THIS CHAPTER IS FOR YOU IF YOU'RE NOT SOMEONE WHO MENSTRUATES, BUT YOU WANT TO BE A GOOD ALLY TO THOSE WHO DO.

LISTEN

If your friend just wants to vent about their period, be a good listener. That is a huge part of just being a good friend in general.

BE SYMPATHETIC

You might not be able to put yourself in our shoes completely, but try.

DON'T ACT LIKE WE'RE DISGUSTING

We're not. Dog poo is disgusting. Cold vomit is disgusting. We're just fine, thank you.

DON'T BLAME OUR BAD MOOD ON PERIODS. MAYBE YOU'RE JUST ANNOYING?

"Have you got your period?" is just the worst question, even if the answer is yes. Never, ever ask it!

BUT YOU CAN STILL (SILENTLY) ACKNOWLEDGE THAT A PERIOD MAY BE MAKING EVERYDAY THINGS TOUGHER FOR US THAN THEY ARE FOR YOU

YOU WILL NEVER KNOW.

WHAT CAN YOU DO INSTEAD?

"What can I do to help?" is one of the greatest questions ever asked. Ask it again. And again. Aaaaand again.

STAND UP FOR US

If someone else is giving us a hard time for reasons beyond our control, your support is absolutely vital and deeply appreciated.

LET OTHER NON-BLEEDERS KNOW WHEN THEY'RE BEING INAPPROPRIATE

Yeah, bullying, shaming and mockery about getting a period actually aren't cool. You may have to call out these behaviours if they're coming from what we call NON-allies. Young boys who are still processing this info may need a little guidance for how to behave. If you can assist, that's less work for the person who's bleeding to have to do.

FORGIVE YOURSELF!

Maybe you were once the kid going, "Ewww, gross" and shrieking at the sight of a pad. That's OK if you've changed. No-one starts out perfect. We all grow and evolve.

YOU MAY NEED TO DO A SUPPLIES RUN

Us: "Can you go to my bag and get a pad?"

You: "Yes. Yes, I can."

PERIODS AND THE ENVIRONMENT

The thing about using ordinary pads and tampons from the supermarket is that they (and all the plastic packaging that comes with them) are disposable ... which means that when you're done with them, they go into landfill. They're not environmentally friendly.

But before you start feeling guilty about polluting the environment with your period, **give yourself a break**. Remember that if you're reading this book, chances are you're relatively new to your period or are still waiting for it to start. Become an expert in managing your period using environmentally sustainable methods only when you're absolutely ready.

So, once you're comfortable being a period boss – how can you reduce your impact on the environment?

Tampons

Most tampons are made of cotton or synthetic rayon, or a combination of both. As a first step, look for organic, pure cotton tampons, as these are better for the environment than tampons where the ingredients are undisclosed. Bear in mind that even 100 per cent organic tampons can take upwards of 100 years to completely break down (although they do break down eventually), and the single-use plastic wrapping they come in can take centuries.

Applicator tampons use up an especially large amount of single-use plastics, so if you're into this method it's better to use brands with cardboard applicators. (To be clear, there's no actual reason applicators are any better than using your fingers to insert a tampon!) You can also find reusable rubber applicators that you wash and carry.

Pads

A plastic, disposable sanitary pad will take between 500 and 800 years to break down in landfill, and wrapping used ones in plastic makes it even harder for them to break down. Thousands of tonnes of disposable sanitary waste are generated every month all over the world!

Don't freak out, though. Look for pads with minimal packaging that don't use bleaching. Recycle their boxes. Once you're comfortable managing your period, you'll probably find you can use smaller pads and fewer of them, or even just liners, to manage the lighter flow days. This will have less impact on the environment.

Period pants

Period pants are great! They're comfortable and reusable, and they last a long time, especially if you wash them using the cold water cycle and gentle soaps and then let them dry in the sun. The only downside is that they're not as effective on the first one to two days of your period, when your flow is heaviest.

Reusable pads

Reusable cloth pads are becoming more popular for environmental reasons, because you throw nothing out. Like period pants, you can wash them in cold water and reuse them for years. They're gaining traction for some people with sensitive skin because, unlike regular pads, they don't contain plastic and have fewer skin irritants.

The downside is that cloth pads can be a little bulky for smaller bodies, and they are not usually sold in supermarkets – so look for them in eco-stores and online.

> To manage my period, I use cloth pads. They're really soft and absorbent. The night-time ones they make really ridiculously huge so you don't get the butt-crack leak! To go out for a full day, I need to take four cloth pads with me, or three if it's my first day. I like to change my pads more often. The pads have little buttons on them, so I usually fold them and click the buttons together and put them back in the bag – used ones roll up neatly like a reusable shopping bag. I have a special bucket and Mum cleans them and dries them on the washing line, leaving them out in the sun for one to two days until they're good and dry. You treat them like nappies – wash them in cold water and don't use the dryer (it shortens their lifespan). They cost between £5 and £15. Lots of little home businesses make them. I like them because they're good for nature, and because we're hippies. *Tans. 13*

Menstrual cups, or 'moon cups', are the most cost-effective and environmentally sensitive way to manage your period, as the cups can be reused for up to 10 years. They do not need to be changed as often as pads and tampons, making them handy for travel and other long commitments, and they create zero waste. They are usually leak-proof and do not emit an odour. The downside is they take some practice getting used to!

The main environmental impact of moon cups is in their production and shipping. Their day-to-day use just requires small amounts of water and soap to clean them. For a lot more on menstrual cups, see page 54.

Free bleeding

Have you ever noticed in TV shows where people are stranded on desert islands, no-one ever talks about managing their periods by free bleeding? Which is weird, because presumably that's what all the people who menstruate are doing, unless they happened to wash up on the island with years' worth of pads and tampons and menstrual cups ...

Free bleeding is the idea of managing your period without any products, just letting the blood flow free. If you're nervous about leakage on to your clothes, this is something to try when you're more familiar with your flow or your cycle is more regular, and you know when your lighter days are likely to be. It's also a good idea to wear darker pants and clothes when you try it.

You can do free bleeding sometimes, like when you're home just chillin', when you know that your flow is really light and will be captured on your underwear (which you can just wash out). You can also do it in the shower – blood just washes down the plughole, which is awesome.

These days there are period activists who advocate for free bleeding throughout your whole cycle. They do this for a number of reasons: because they believe that we shouldn't be ashamed of menstruating (which is true – nearly half the population do it regularly!), or because they feel more comfortable bleeding on to their clothes than capturing the blood on a pad, tampon or cup. Some are also trying to create less waste and landfill by avoiding disposable period products.

ABOUT THE VAGINA

The vagina is important enough to get its own chapter in this book.

A lot of kids aren't aware that they even have a vagina until they are older. (They just know about wee holes and poo holes.) This is totally normal! Most kids haven't had to deal with it much.

But as you get older, you'll develop a sense that it's there. Around puberty you will start to have a clear or milky discharge from your vagina. Sexy feelings or thoughts may loop back to that area, too. It's all normal and part of growing up. (For more on discharge, see page 60.)

How can I see my vagina?

Standing in front of a mirror in the nude won't actually help you see it – it's in a spot that's tricky to see front-on.

The best way to see your vagina is to crouch down and hold a hand-mirror between your legs. You could also lie on your back with your head propped up on a pillow, and bend your knees up before trying to see it with the mirror.

To see the opening of the vagina, you'll need to use your fingers to separate the outer labia, or lips, which come together over the vaginal opening. Even then, you might not be able to see much.

When the vagina is resting, its walls often touch each other. You can put your clean finger in gently to separate the walls and try to look further in.

THE VAGINA IS A TUBE OF MUSCLE THAT GROWS BIGGER DURING PUBERTY AND DEVELOPS A SOFT, SPONGY LINING.

People mistakenly refer to all their 'bits' as a 'vagina' but the whole part of you that fits inside your underpants is called the 'vulva'. The vagina is just the tube between your vulva and your cervix.

The cervix is part of the uterus, but it's narrow and has only a small, slit-like opening between your uterus and the rest of the world. (During childbirth, this small opening expands massively under the influence of special hormones.) It's difficult to get beyond the cervix without being a doctor – but when you have your period, blood travels through your cervix from your uterus and into your vagina.

Puberty?
I'm a big fan!

You won't get your period unless you're going through puberty – it's part of a package deal.

Puberty involves lots of amazing changes inside your body and out. It's nature's way of getting your body ready to be able to reproduce. It can definitely feel as though an alien has taken over. Thanks to a heap of new hormones, puberty makes your body do weird stuff like sprout underarm and pubic hair and change proportions. Puberty can also send you into emotional spin-outs. But if you think about it, puberty is also pretty awesome. How cool is it that your body just starts changing you into the adult version of yourself – without an instruction manual!

What a rollercoaster!

My son has been a massive *Alice in Wonderland* fan all his life (he even had an *Alice*-themed tea party for his 16th birthday). Some of Alice's adventures remind me of what puberty can feel like – like when her body suddenly grows and shrinks after she takes a bite of cake or has a sip of cordial, and it just feels out of control. *Dr Melissa*

Help! I just hit puberty

Puberty can feel sudden and unstoppable – even though it's actually been on its way for quite a long time. It's as if you've been floating gently down a river, and then you suddenly hit a waterfall! You may not know it, but the growth spurt and change in your body 'hit' one to two years before your first period. And *when* they hit is different for everyone.

Random puberty facts

⭐ All animals – from alligators to bees to humans to salmon to zebra finches – go through some sort of puberty.

⭐ During puberty, you will grow faster than at any other time in your life (except your first two years).

⭐ On average, people get taller by around 25 per cent during puberty!

⭐ Your arms get proportionately longer, and because your body grows, your head gets proportionately smaller.

⭐ The brain grows only a little in size during puberty, but goes through massive changes to its different parts and electrical circuits.

- Changes in the brain's 'wiring' in puberty help with things like problem-solving, hand–eye coordination, understanding emotions better, and being able to think about and 'get' where another person is coming from.

Other stuff that happens in puberty

These are the obvious ones, because you can see them.

- You'll grow breasts and pubic hair.

- Skin and hair get more oily, which contributes to spots.

- Armpits grow hair, as well as developing a type of sweat gland that attracts skin bacteria that cause BO (body odour).

- Your body shape changes partly because of your bone 'architecture' and the way muscles and fat are arranged. Your weight also increases due to everything growing. (To be fair, you've been growing and changing your whole life, but puberty just speeds things up a bit!)

Everyone's body is different, and puberty is different for everyone. Height and weight, skin and hair colour, individual facial features, genitals, body shapes and sizes – there are amazing variations even within families.

During puberty your brain changes, which has an effect on your thoughts and feelings. You might feel overly emotional – super angry or sad, or anything in between – for no reason. You might start to feel self-conscious, or worry that your body is weird compared with everyone else's. (You also might not, in which case – yay!)

If you do feel self-conscious, try to remember that feeling like you're a freak – or uncoordinated, or hideous – will definitely pass, and it's also not true. No matter what is happening to your body, you are fine the way you are. Your brain is just Going Through Some Stuff.

On the plus side, those brain changes also mean that we develop the ability to start seeing things from another person's point of view. So, try to remember that everyone around you is going through the same thing, and different things, at different times. It's kind of amazing!

FUN FACT ABOUT PERIODS

The only animals that have periods are humans, apes, monkeys, elephant shrews, bats and – as recently discovered – the spiny mouse. Other animals have similar hormone cycles, but they absorb their uterus lining internally – it doesn't flow outside the body.

IS SOMETHING WRONG?

Periods happen naturally for most of us who are born with ovaries, a uterus and vagina. For some, stuff happens that makes us think something's wrong. Many teenage girls who wrote to me as Dolly Doctor about their periods were worried there was a problem. I always hoped to be able to reassure them. Sometimes I thought there might be an issue and would recommend getting a check-up from a doctor. But most of the time, medical causes of period problems in teenagers are common and easy enough to manage.

My best friend in high school didn't start puberty until she was almost 14, and her periods didn't start until she was 16. She remained petite while the rest of the girls got taller and grew curves. The thing I remember most is how mean some of the kids at school were. They called her nicknames and snickered quietly so that she could hear but the teachers couldn't. And the worst thing was – this came from other girls. Even though these girls liked her too; she was a really lovely person, popular with the boys, smart and caring! Being humiliated like this was her private agony for those first three and a half years of high school.

Having a really amazing mum helped her get through some of that pain, and I hope that having good friends (like me!) also helped. But what is it with the need to be mean to people who are on a different timeline to you? Being mean is the opposite of anything even remotely cool. *Dr Melissa*

My period hasn't come yet

> **I'm 15 and haven't got my period yet. My sister who is two years younger than me has got hers. Is there something wrong with me?**

When those around you get their period, and you don't, it can be kind of awesome at first – the longer you can put off dealing with pads, bleeding and PMS, the better!

Then months go by and maybe you start thinking, 'Is something wrong with me?'

The easiest way to reassure yourself is to check the rest of your body's changes. Remember: puberty is so much more than periods! See page 122 for more.

✦ How much taller have you grown in the past two years?

★ Have your breasts and pubic hair developed a little or a lot?

★ Have you noticed more subtle things, like your voice deepening a bit and more facial and body hair? (This happens very noticeably in boys, but girls get this too.)

Periods begin late in puberty, when most of the above changes are well underway. It's usually at least two years after breast development before you can expect your first period.

The timing of puberty (your age when it first starts) is partly controlled by your genes – so if your mother or older sisters were older than average to start, chances are you will be too. From a medical point of view, we recommend a check-up if:

⭐ Your breasts started growing by age 10 or earlier, but you have not started your periods by the age of 14.

⭐ Your breasts started growing at age 14 but you have not started your periods by the age of 16.

If either of these scenarios sounds like you, there's still no need to panic. You could be among that small percentage of people whose natural puberty timeline is just a little later.

Reasons for getting your period after everyone else

There are medical and physical conditions that cause a delay or an absence of periods. One of the more common reasons is excessive exercise. Another is insufficient nutrition, which can be due to an eating disorder or poverty, or living in a country where drought, war or other causes of food insecurity have led to famine.

Most of the other causes relate to hormonal problems and it can take a bunch of hormone tests to work out what's going on. The hormone tests are organized by doctors, using a blood sample.

(Don't be freaked out by this – it's easy for a nurse to take a blood sample from one of the veins in the crook of the elbow – they're big and close to the surface. There's a small needle sting, but you can handle it.)

Other causes are genetic conditions that mean that one part of the menstrual cycle control centres (from the brain to the ovaries) never gets programmed to kick off.

Very rarely, the vagina and uterus are absent from birth. This might go undetected even after puberty, and only comes to light when the absence of periods causes the patient to see a doctor.

Finally, your period can come late if there has been an earlier medical condition such as cancer in childhood. Treatments involving chemotherapy or radiotherapy affect the organs that control puberty and periods, and this can affect physical development later on.

How do I talk to a doctor about this?

If you're thinking of going to your doctor to talk about your period starting late, the conversation might go like this:

Me: "I'm worried about the fact that I haven't got my period yet. I'm XX years old. All my friends have got their period."

How old was your mother when she got her period? What about your older sisters?

OK, can I ask you a few questions about puberty? That will help us figure out when we might expect your periods. When did you notice your breasts growing? What about pubic hair? Have you had a growth spurt? Have you noticed discharge or fluid in your pants? For how long?

Now some questions about your general health. Has your weight changed much in recent months? Have you changed the type or amount of food you eat? What about exercise – what's an average week like? Ever had any chronic or serious illnesses?

Then the doctor might weigh you, measure your height and show you a diagram of puberty development and ask you where you think your body is at. From there, they should be able to give you some advice or reassurance.

My periods are really irregular

66 I was wondering, is it normal not to get your period every 28 days? I'm 16 years old and sometimes it's late, like every 30 days, and sometimes it's early, like 26 or 27 days. Is this normal? 99

66 I'm 15 and I first got my period when I was 12. It was on a normal cycle every month, then it started to come between three and six months, and then about six months ago I had my period for one week for three months, and then it just stopped again. I know cycles take a while to adjust, but this just feels weird. 99

Periods really ARE confusing! Sometimes. You wait and wait for that first period, it finally arrives – yay! You're a master menstruator! Then … *nothing happens.*

You might be wondering if: (a) it was all a dream, (b) it was a false start and you're being tricked! or (c) something really bad is going on. But chances are, everything's fine – it's really common for your period to be irregular for the first couple of years.

After two years from the very first period, most girls will fall into a regular period pattern, called the 'menstrual cycle'. (See page 148 for how the menstrual cycle works.)

The cycle is counted in days, from the first day of one period to the first day of the next period. The cycle does not have to be EXACTLY the same each time: it can vary from between 22 and 45 days when you're a teenager, to between 22 and 35 days once your body's finished all its growing.

In the letter from the sixteen-year-old, the menstrual cycle that varies from 26 to 30 days is considered completely regular.

On the other hand, the fifteen-year-old who wrote in might be experiencing irregular cycles, since it's been more than two years since her first period and she might be having cycles lasting more than 45 days.

A really helpful way to track your cycle is to use a period tracker app for a few months. It helps guide you and your doctor as to whether any tests need to be done.

If your cycle has been regular but has become irregular after two to three years, or if it has NEVER been regular and it's been more than two years since your first period, then it could be time to get a check-up.

A common cause of periods becoming irregular is stress. It's difficult to say how much stress is 'too much', because everyone responds to stress differently. But being significantly stressed over time – due to study, school, family or friend issues – can be enough to influence the pattern of your periods. Changes to your eating patterns or weight can also change the regularity of your cycle.

In teenagers, truly irregular periods are often caused by hormone imbalances or problems. The most common of these is a condition called polycystic ovary syndrome, or PCOS (see page 142).

QUESTIONS FOR DR MELISSA

My periods have stopped. Am I pregnant?

❝ I'm really worried about my period. I've missed a full month and it's going on to the second month now and I'm scared something's wrong with me. I've never had sex but can I be pregnant? ❞

If you've never had sex, then no, you can't be pregnant.

It's totally normal for your mind to 'go there' when you miss a period, because we're often taught that missed periods = pregnancy. But there are lots of reasons why you can miss a period that have nothing to do with pregnancy.

It might help you to remember that there are only a few ways pregnancy can happen:

★ The most common way is from sexual intercourse (penis-in-vagina sex). During unprotected sex, fluid called 'semen' is squirted out from a guy's penis into the vagina. This is called ejaculation. Semen contains sperm. If sperm fertilizes the egg, that can result in pregnancy. (See page 136.)

⭐ Sometimes the guy pulls out his penis before he ejaculates, and squirts his semen outside the vagina. Fluid containing sperm can still have leaked inside the vagina before the final squirt, where it can travel up the vagina to fertilize an egg.

If there has not been unprotected sex where the guy ejaculated inside the vagina, but you have been intimate with someone, you could fall pregnant the following ways:

⭐ He's wearing a condom but it breaks or slips off during intercourse. Therefore the sex was unprotected, so semen could be present and may fertilize an egg.

⭐ Sometimes there's semen close to the opening of the vagina, even if the penis didn't go all the way inside it. Sperm are good swimmers and in the right conditions, they can travel up towards the uterus and, *very rarely*, fertilize an egg. This is a low-risk situation, and the semen would have to physically touch the opening of the vagina where it's moist – it won't swim on your outside skin.

In these scenarios, pregnancy is possible. Not *likely*, just possible.

If NONE of these scenarios have happened and a sperm has never been near your body, let alone *inside* of your body, then pregnancy is <u>not possible.</u>

WHAT IS PERIOD POVERTY?

Period poverty is not being able to afford menstrual products. It affects people in every country – rich countries and poor countries, including your own. Period poverty happens when other needs – for example, the need for food or shelter – come before spending money on menstrual products. Being in that situation has big implications. For young girls, period poverty might mean they cannot attend school.

More and more, people are recognizing that period poverty is an important cause of inequality. There is a global push to make menstrual products free. Some countries are removing the 'Tampon Tax', to ensure that tampons and other menstrual products are classified as 'essential items' by the government, rather than 'luxury items' that do get taxed. Lots of young kids have been involved in the protesting of this tax.

Another reason that some people don't have access to menstrual products is the stigma associated with periods. Stigma is a negative attitude or feeling (such as shame or disgrace) cast over people for something they are or something they have done. Stigma can be so powerful that it can leave people feeling isolated or depressed. Sadly, there are still a lot of beliefs about periods that make it impossible for people who are menstruating to be part of a community. But no one should ever feel ashamed about having periods!

PERIODS AND SEX

Most readers will not be at this point in their lives yet but come back when you're ready. Knowledge is power!

Can you have sex while you have your period?

Yes, if you wanted to! It's the same as sex at any other time of your menstrual cycle, except you would need to remove your tampon or menstrual cup first, and there would be some blood to wipe up afterwards.

Is it possible to get pregnant while you're menstruating?

Yes, you can get pregnant during your period. Having your period does not rule out the risk of pregnancy, as sperm can live for up to five days inside the uterus and Fallopian tubes. And sometimes you can ovulate early in your menstrual cycle. If you don't want to risk pregnancy, use protection such as condoms, or find out about other types of contraception. Condoms have the added bonus of protecting against sexually transmitted infections.

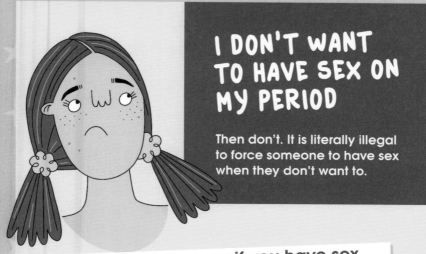

I DON'T WANT TO HAVE SEX ON MY PERIOD

Then don't. It is literally illegal to force someone to have sex when they don't want to.

What happens if you have sex without removing your tampon?

Whoops! This isn't ideal, since they get pushed up high, which makes it harder to remove them, and it might feel uncomfortable.

If you have accidentally left a tampon in, make sure you take it out straight after sex. If you have any problems getting it out, it's OK to go to the doctor and ask for help removing it. But don't freak out – this has happened literally millions of times before. **You will be OK.**

My periods are super heavy

66 Hey ... this might seem a bit crude, but my periods are really heavy ... and there are these huge blobs throughout it! Is this normal?? I've only had my period for six months 😟 Is that unusual? 99

It can be difficult to know when your period is 'too heavy'. After all, if the first couple of days of your period require pad or tampon changes every two to three hours, and you're trying to get through a school day or enjoy a long movie, that can seem heavy enough, thanks very much!

But sometimes periods can be too heavy. Blobs and clots are pretty normal, but medical guidelines say that a person has 'heavy menstrual bleeding' when their periods are heavy enough to interfere with their physical, social, emotional or material quality of life.

In other words, when consistent, heavy or prolonged periods regularly get in the way of going out, study, hobbies, activities and having fun, or if they are causing physical complications such as iron deficiency, then they meet the medical definition of 'heavy'.

HOW HEAVY IS TOO HEAVY?

If your periods are lasting longer than eight days every month, or you have to change pads or tampons every hour, or you get up through the night on most nights of your period to change tampons or pads, or you're having blood clots that are larger than a 50 pence piece – then your period is too heavy, and it's worth talking to your doctor about your options.

Why do some people get periods that are too heavy?

The causes of 'heavy menstrual bleeding' are often different for adolescents than for older women (such as your mum). For adolescents, here are the causes of heavy periods – listed roughly in order from most common to least:

🌟 **Going through puberty**: In adolescents, heavy bleeding can be due to hormonal fluctuations and imbalances, which are part of the puberty chain that can also cause periods to disappear. (I told you it was confusing!)

⭐ **Polycystic ovary syndrome (PCOS):** There is a condition, known as polycystic ovary syndrome (PCOS), that can cause irregular periods, and these periods can be light or really heavy. (More on PCOS on page 142).

⭐ **Thyroid gland problems:** An underactive thyroid gland is a less common cause of heavy periods. The thyroid gland is a small, fleshy gland that sits at the front of your neck below your voice box. It makes hormones that help control your body's metabolism and the way your body uses its fuel (food and nutrition) to expend energy. This might not seem to have much to do with periods, but in fact all the hormone systems in the body interact in some way with each other. If something goes wrong with the thyroid gland, it can affect your periods.

★ **A problem with the blood-clotting system:** A rare cause of heavy bleeding in adolescents is a problem with the body's blood-clotting system. Imagine that you cut your finger; it will bleed, but within a few minutes the bleeding stops and forms a blood clot. During a period, tiny blood vessels in the lining of the uterus leak blood while the lining sheds. Like bleeding from a skin cut, the usual blood-clotting mechanism in the body kicks in during a period so that these

blood vessels don't leak indefinitely. However, there are medical conditions (such as a genetic clotting disorder) where a person's blood clots too much, or not enough.

★ **Growths inside the uterus:** Problems inside the uterus can cause heavy menstrual bleeding. There are a few types of growths that affect the muscle layer of the uterus, or the lining itself, which can lead to bleeding. These usually affect older women and are extremely rare in adolescents.

★ **Pregnancy:** This would go to the top of the list if you were sexually active. Even though pregnancy usually causes periods to stop (see page 133), bleeding during pregnancy can be a sign of a miscarriage, which is not uncommon. If pregnancy is possible, it's easy to rule it out as the cause for heavy bleeding with a simple test.

★ **No obvious cause:** Sometimes, girls have heavy menstrual bleeding and nothing turns up in any of the tests. Heavy bleeding in this situation is thought to be related to a disturbance of the way blood would normally start to clot inside the lining of the uterus when it sheds during a period.

WHAT HAPPENS IF I HAVE REALLY HEAVY PERIODS?

It's often helpful to bring the heavy bleeding under control using medication to stop the regular blood loss. Losing too much blood each month can lead to iron deficiency, which can cause tiredness and difficulty concentrating.

It's good to see a doctor, who will look into the possible causes and might do blood tests and maybe an ultrasound to look at the ovaries and uterus.

Polycystic ovary syndrome (PCOS)

> **I'm a 15-year-old girl and I get excessive hair on my face and body, a lot of pimples on my back and quite a few on my face, and irregular periods. Could this mean I have a hormonal imbalance? If I got the problem fixed by going on the Pill would the excessive hair and pimples go away? Please help!**

PCOS is something that affects quite a lot of people, but I want to give you one piece of advice right upfront: if you look stuff up on the internet about PCOS, make sure: (a) it's a trustworthy source and (b) the information you read is relevant to teenagers.

PCOS looks different in adolescents than in adults – the reason being that it can take the body at least two years to find its own pattern of menstrual cycles. So please remember: the information on the internet can make a whole lot of teenagers worry for nothing!

WHAT IS PCOS?

PCOS is a condition where there are certain interactions between the menstrual hormones and other hormones in the body, including testosterone (one of the sex hormones that's much higher in males) and insulin, which is related to controlling sugar levels in the bloodstream.

A useful way to think of PCOS is as a kind of hormone imbalance. This imbalance leads to a bunch of symptoms. PCOS affects about one per cent of teenagers, but the percentage increases with being overweight or obese.

How do you know if you have PCOS?

Diagnosing PCOS is different for adolescents and adults. In adults, PCOS is diagnosed by having irregular periods, excessive body hair or acne, and seeing lots of mini-cysts on the ovaries on an ultrasound. Cysts are fluid-filled pouches. Throughout adolescence, the ovaries are still maturing and naturally have what looks like lots of little 'cysts'. These can get mistaken for being polycystic (aka 'lots of cysts') when they're not. Therefore, an ultrasound of the ovaries should NOT be done on adolescents to diagnose PCOS.

So there are different criteria if you're a teenager:

⭐ 'Irregular' periods in adolescents: if it's been about three years since the very first period, and periods are more than 35 days or less than 21 days apart, they are defined as irregular.

⭐ Signs of excessive testosterone-like hormone effects on the skin: excessive body or facial hair, persistent acne that's hard to treat or hair loss on the scalp.

What happens if you have PCOS?

Adults with PCOS tend not to ovulate regularly, which impacts on their fertility. They often have difficulty with weight control and can be overweight. This can lead to problems with the way their body's insulin works, and therefore affect blood sugar.

The recommended treatment for adolescents with PCOS is the Pill, which restores some of the hormone imbalance and the symptoms associated with this. Regular exercise and weight management might also be important. Depending on sugar and insulin levels in the blood, other treatment might also be recommended.

IF YOU'RE WORRIED THAT YOU HAVE PCOS, OR WANT TO LEARN MORE, START BY VISITING YOUR DOCTOR.

Tampons and toxic shock syndrome

I heard about something called TSS? Is there a way to treat it?

Toxic shock syndrome (TSS) is caused by a particular type of bacterial infection where the bacteria (germs) produce a toxin.

TSS is extremely rare. The infection can happen in other parts of the body, and can affect anyone (children, adults, men ... not just bleeders), but TSS was associated with the use of super-absorbent tampons (which are no longer available), especially when left inside the vagina for several hours, allowing the bacteria to multiply and release a toxin. Symptoms are usually a high fever, vomiting, diarrhoea, a rash, muscle aches and headaches. If it is not treated, TSS can lead to 'shock' – a drop in blood pressure, confusion and kidney failure.

TSS is a medical emergency and must be treated in hospital with intravenous antibiotics and fluids. Changing tampons at least every four hours and washing hands before and after changing your tampon are great ways to prevent TSS. Some people find it helps to set an alarm on their phone.

My periods are so painful they affect my daily life

66 When I get my period I have unbearable pains ... I can't do anything and I get very sick. I've seen my doctor and she thinks the blood is goin' back up through the Fallopian tubes. 99

66 I'm 15 and have had my period since I was 11. I'm always in constant pain throughout the whole week of my period. I have gone to my doctor and got prescription pills to help with the pain but they don't seem to work. 99

First of all, sorry that you're going through this. It's no fun.

It might help to know you're not alone: About 10 per cent of adolescents with period pain experience it with such severity that they regularly miss school, work and other activities.

This is totally rubbish!

There might not be an underlying cause and there are treatments that do help (see page 93).

Any period pain that causes life to come to a grinding halt, or is simply unbearable, deserves to be thoroughly checked out. Feel confident that what you're experiencing does not have to be your life – a doctor will be able to help.

To fully arm yourself, keep track of your symptoms and where they sit on your monthly cycle (see 'Keeping Track', page 58) and bring this info along to your appointment. Also be prepared to push back on well-meaning parents or carers who tell you that "this is normal" or "you just have to suck it up".

It's sometimes hard to know what you're feeling when it's new – talking to your friends or trusted grown-ups can really help you figure it out!

Endometriosis

Endometriosis is a common condition in which the tissue that is similar to the lining of the uterus grows outside it in other parts of the body. It affects five to ten per cent of teenagers and young women. The most common symptom is pain – period pain that doesn't get better with painkillers or prescription treatment, pain that persists for days, pain that can come at other times of the menstrual cycle but feels like period pain (without the bleeding).

Endometriosis is a very individual condition, but some people have chronic pain that's awful and doesn't go away with the usual treatments (see page 96). If you suspect that you might have endometriosis, talk to your doctor right away, so that they can figure out how to help you.

I grew up in a small country town and all the doctors were friends with my dad. There was NO WAY that I wanted their advice on periods, nor did I want to be in any situation where they'd be looking at my vagina. I GET IT, TRUST ME, I GET IT. So here's the thing: you're growing up, and that means you're being put in charge of your body. You're the boss! To run her body well, the boss needs good advice, and good advice comes from a good GP. Bosses can't go it alone, so even though it might feel strange right now, get a doctor, have their number in your phone or diary, and if you need to chat, make the call. Doctors must keep information confidential (unless you are in immediate danger). *Yumi*

THE INCREDIBLE MONTHLY HORMONE CYCLE

This book is mainly about getting your period, but the whole menstrual cycle is also pretty cool!

TIP We count the first day of your period as Day One of your cycle.

What goes on in a monthly hormone (menstrual) cycle?

Remember how we talked about why people get periods? It's the body's way of preparing for a future pregnancy. The menstrual cycle is a lot about that preparation. To help get our heads around it, we divide the menstrual cycle into two halves, or 'phases'.

In the first half, hormones from the brain are signalling the ovaries to make more hormones that will ripen an egg.

In the second half, after the ripened egg is released (known as 'ovulation'), there's a small window of time during which the lining of the uterus waits for that egg to be fertilized by sperm (this is known as 'conception').

If conception doesn't happen – and most of the time it doesn't, because we are not pregnant very often – hormone levels adjust again. Then, around two weeks after ovulation, the lining sheds and THAT'S when you get your period.

PHASE 1: Egg-ripening

There's actually a competition that goes on each month: a few eggs-to-be are contenders, and they begin the ripening process. But by about day eight of the cycle, one egg has dominated. It gets to ripen fully, and it is the one to travel to the uterus on around day 14–16 (depending on the length of your cycle – it's often longer in younger teens). Eggs are very tiny – about the size of the full stop at the end of this line.

To help this process, there is a rapid increase in the level of oestrogen, one of the main menstrual-cycle hormones. Oestrogen helps with egg-ripening and preparing the lining of the uterus, but it also changes the texture of the mucus that's made by your cervix. The mucus becomes thin, runny and clear and you might notice this more than other discharge throughout the month – mainly because it's runnier.

PHASE 2: POP! goes the egg

Your egg has been ripening in its own special 'house', also known as the ovary. When that house gets all the right signals, it 'opens the door' and lets the egg out. This is called **ovulation**. Some people feel a sharp pain when this happens, and some might even notice a spot of blood. It's usually very short-lived. Some people experience an increase in sex drive around the time of ovulation, and it's thought that this is to encourage the creation of babies.

The egg's journey

Once an egg has popped, it only has a couple of days to live ... unless it meets a sperm. Fertilisation (when the egg and sperm meet) is the very first step in making a baby. Most eggs – whether they're the ones in the ovaries or the ones that pop once puberty is underway – do **NOT** make babies. That is nature's course. Same with sperm – millions get made, but almost all don't go on to make babies.

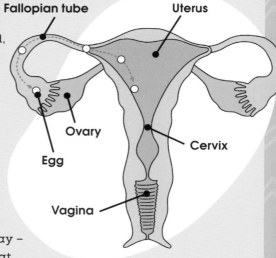

If an egg is not fertilized, it simply dissolves inside the Fallopian tube.

Once the egg has popped

After ovulation – the release of the ripened egg by the ovary – the level of oestrogen dramatically drops for about a week, but then picks up again a little bit. At the same time, another type of menstrual hormone, progesterone, increases. Progesterone makes the mucus from the cervix thick and sticky, and this can make it seem like you have a different discharge when really it's all coming from the same place.

The 'premenstrual' blues

Research has looked at how the menstrual hormones affect our emotions, thoughts and moods. The dip in oestrogen and rise in progesterone in the second half of the menstrual cycle seem to have an effect on mood for some people. Many people feel irritable, depressed or anxious before they menstruate, or have trouble regulating emotions – and this can lead to fights or feelings of grumpiness towards others.

Other premenstrual symptoms related to hormones include breast tenderness, bloating, weight gain, headaches, food cravings, increased appetite and joint and muscle pains.

The big clue to figuring out if these are related to the menstrual cycle is if the symptoms only appear after ovulation, and DISAPPEAR when your period starts. See page 92 for information on premenstrual syndrome (PMS).

PERIOD BOSS *Pledge*

All Period Bosses know: **KNOWLEDGE IS POWER!** The more info you have about your period, the better.

A Period Boss **DOES NOT JUDGE** how other people manage their periods. If you prefer pads, tampons, period pants or whatever, that's fine. Your body. Your choice. Zero judging.

A Period Boss understands that being 'grossed out' by periods is babyish and helps no-one.

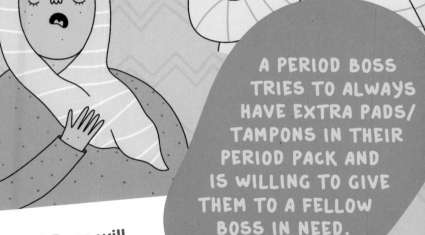

A PERIOD BOSS TRIES TO ALWAYS HAVE EXTRA PADS/ TAMPONS IN THEIR PERIOD PACK AND IS WILLING TO GIVE THEM TO A FELLOW BOSS IN NEED.

A Period Boss will dutifully perform a pants check for leaks if asked. Even if asked by a total stranger.

153

EXPAND YOUR PERIOD VOCABULARY!

BLOOD CLOT

A clump of blood that has become solid – a bit like jelly – that sometimes comes out during your period.

APPLICATOR

A plastic or a cardboard tube that comes with some tampons and might help with tampon insertion.

CERVIX

The lower, narrower part of the uterus.

CONTRACEPTIVE

Something that is intended to stop pregnancy. Can take many forms – condom, the rod, IUD and the Pill, to name a few.

CRAMP

A painful muscle spasm that can occur during your period.

CYCLE

Refers to the menstrual cycle – once you start getting your period, you will always be at one point in your cycle.